GRAPHICACY AND GEOGRAPHY TEACHING

Graphicacy
and Geography Teaching

DAVID BOARDMAN

66805

CROOM HELM
London & Canberra

© 1983 David Boardman
Croom Helm Ltd, Provident House, Burrell Row,
Beckenham, Kent BR3 1AT

British Library Cataloguing in Publication Data

Boardman, David
  Graphicacy and geography teaching.
  1. Geography — Study and teaching
  I. Title
  910'.7   G76

ISBN 0-7099-0644-7

Printed in Great Britain by
Biddles Ltd, Guildford, Surrey

Contents

Figures

Preface

Graphicacy is the most distinctively geographical form of
communication. It is essentially the communication of spatial
information through maps and other forms of illustration. In
geography this kind of information cannot be communicated
effectively by means of words or numbers alone.

The word literacy has been in use for a long time to
describe communication by means of written language. More
recently the word oracy has been used to indicate facility
with spoken language. The term numeracy to describe communication through mathematical symbols, often regarded as the
most refined form of language, has been universally adopted to
describe competence with numbers. An educated person is
expected to be both literate and numerate.

The term graphicacy was first proposed in an influential
article by Balchin and Coleman (1965) who argued that it should
be 'the fourth ace in the pack'. They noted the need for a
word which describes the communication of spatial relationships,
as in the plan of a house, the layout of a farm, the map of a
village, the route through a town, the sketch of a landform,
or the photograph of a landscape. The common route of the words
cartography, photography and other forms of graphic communication is used as the stem of the word graphicacy. Balchin and
Coleman describe literacy, numeracy, articulacy (subsequently
superseded by oracy) and graphicacy as the four 'acies', or
'aces' for short.

Graphicacy became part of every geography teacher's
vocabulary after Professor Balchin used the word as the title
of his presidential address to the Geographical Association in
1972. On this occasion he defined graphicacy precisely as
'the communication of spatial information that cannot be conveyed adequately by verbal or numerical means' (Balchin, 1972).
Here 'verbal' was taken as meaning the written as distinct
from the spoken word.

Balchin's main argument is that the concept of graphicacy gives geography its essential ethos. He refers to the incoming process as map reading and interpretation, and the outgoing process as map making and drawing. He recommends that teaching which includes the development of graphicacy in children should begin in primary schools. Visual-spatial ability is evident in young children, who draw simple pictures before they learn to read or write. This emerging visual-spatial ability should be fostered through carefully structured and sequenced teaching. Balchin concludes that effective geography teaching should utilise and integrate literacy, numeracy, articulacy (oracy) and graphicacy. Neither words nor numbers nor drawings are superior or inferior as modes of communication. They are only more suitable or less suitable for particular purposes, and each ranges from the very simple to the extremely complex. They complement each other and achieve their highest level of communication when properly integrated.

Progress in graphicacy was reported in a further article by Balchin and Coleman (1973) and in another article written as a contribution to the 'great debate' on education, Balchin (1977) noted the general agreement that a greater effort should be made to ensure that all future citizens acquire certain essential skills before they leave school. He observed that discussion was clouded, however, by the tendency of educationists to argue either from traditional premises such as the three Rs, or from the standpoint of the established subject disciplines. Balchin argued that the discussion ought to be more concerned with modes of communication and that the three Rs should be replaced by the 'four aces'. He also noted that in France a similar discussion was taking place around the concept of 'four languages' in communication skills and the need to teach them to all pupils. These four languages corresponded exactly with the four modes of communication distinguished in Britain.

Meanwhile it had been argued by Boardman (1976a) that geography teachers share with their colleagues in other subjects, especially English and Mathematics, responsibility for ensuring that graphicacy is developed by all pupils before they leave school. He emphasised that perceptual ability and the development of spatial concepts are crucial to the meaningful study of maps and photographs. He recommended a structured programme of study utilising these documents and provided a worked example of a programme used with secondary pupils (Boardman, 1976b). The Social Science Research Council subsequently supported a study of graphicacy in school leavers (Boardman and Towner, 1979, 1980).

PREFACE

The recognition of graphicacy as the strong and distinctive contribution of geography to the school curriculum is reaffirmed in a statement issued by the Geographical Association (1981) as a response to the curriculum debate promoted by the Department of Education and Science. This statement, published as a leaflet and distributed to all local education authorities in England and Wales for circulation to schools, emphasises that graphicacy is a crucially important contribution of geography to the school curriculum for pupils of all ages from 5 to 16. Only in geography are pupils taught systematically to read and use maps. Aspects of graphicacy are discussed in the Association's handbooks on geographical work in primary and middle schools (Mills, 1981) and on geographical education in secondary schools (Graves, 1980). Graphicacy provides part of the framework for an advisory document on the study of place in the primary school produced by the Inner London Education Authority (1981). Education for graphicacy is implicit in a volume reviewing developments in school geography during the 1970s and pointing the way to developments in the 1980s (Walford, 1981).

Ten years after the word graphicacy became commonly used by geography teachers seems an opportune time for the publication of the first book incorporating the term into its title. An attempt to provide a theoretical underpinning for the concept is made in the first chapter of the present volume by using the stages of intellectual development identified in children by Jean Piaget and his associates, whose work has been influential in education. This is followed by a chapter outlining some of the studies which have been undertaken into the problems that pupils encounter in reading and using maps and photographs. Methods of teaching essential concepts and skills of graphicacy to primary, middle and lower secondary school children are discussed in Chapters 3 and 4. The kinds of work which older pupils may be expected to attempt with Ordnance Survey maps, the most complex documents that they are likely to study in geography lessons, are reviewed in Chapters 5 and 6. Fieldwork, an integral part of the development of graphicacy, is illustrated by means of four case studies in the penultimate chapter, whilst the final chapter considers the role of the computer as an aid to learning, probably the most far reaching development of the 1980s. The Appendix lists 100 graphicacy skills and suggests the approximate ages at which pupils of average ability should normally be able to achieve them.

Acknowledgements

This introductory book on graphicacy is written for teachers
of geography and environmental studies in primary, middle and
secondary schools, and for student teachers taking P.G.C.E.
and B.Ed. courses. Over the years many teachers, students and
pupils have taught me a great deal about the complexities of
map reading and interpretation in the classroom and in the
field.

Although these kind people are too numerous to mention
here, I should like to acknowledge the generous help I have
received from three in particular. Elizabeth Towner, Research
Fellow at the University of Birmingham, carried out with me
the study of graphicacy in school leavers which was financed
by the Social Science Research Council. Joy Palmer, Head of
Environmental Studies at Chivenor Primary School, Birmingham,
introduced me to teaching top juniors and organised the fieldwork on a housing estate in Birmingham and a farm in Devon.
My colleague Roger Robinson, Lecturer in Education at the
University of Birmingham, has been a constant source of ideas
and has guided me in the use of the computer.

Figures 4.3 and 4.10 are reproduced from Ordnance Survey
maps with the permission of the Controller of Her Majesty's
Stationery Office, Crown copyright reserved. The following
illustrations are also reproduced by permission: Figure 4.9,
Graveley of Birmingham; Figures 6.1 and 6.2, the Joint
Matriculation Board; Figures 7.3 and 7.4, the Harborne Society;
Figures 7.5 and 7.6, Pamela Green; Figure 8.1, the Schools
Council and Longman; Figures 8.2 and 8.3, Longman Resources
Unit.

Finally, my warmest thanks are due to Frances Saul, who
meticulously and efficiently prepared the manuscript for
publication.

David Boardman

1 The Foundations of Graphicacy

The concept of graphicacy requires an understanding of children's spatial concept development. Investigations into the stages of development in children's thinking carried out by Jean Piaget and his associates in Geneva, spanning more than half a century, exceed those of any other psychologist. His work has many important educational implications and has greatly influenced the work of teachers in both primary and secondary schools. Piaget's theory and approach have stood up well to the test of time and his findings have been confirmed by other workers who have replicated his experiments. Although some of his views are not universally accepted and there have been other analyses of spatial ability such as that of MacFarlane-Smith (1964), Piaget has provided the only comprehensive theory of spatial concept development which can be directly applied to the study of maps. In this chapter a summary of Piaget's stages of children's intellectual development, the best known aspect of his work, is followed by an attempt to relate these stages to children's understanding of topological, projective and Euclidean space. It is necessary to emphasise, however, that this is a brief and simplified account of what is to psychologists a highly complex and still not fully understood subject. For a full discussion of children's spatial concept development reference should be made to the original works of Piaget and his associates (Piaget and Inhelder, 1956; Piaget, Inhelder and Szeminska, 1960). Since much of Piaget's writing is difficult to follow, the reader who requires further details of his work is referred to more accessible accounts such as those of Beard (1969), Brearley and Hitchfield (1966), Furth (1970), Richmond (1970) and McNally (1973).

Intellectual Development

Piaget's theory of the development of children's thinking is based on hundreds of experiments using what is generally called the 'clinical' method. It involves conversations with each individual child and these differ according to the replies given by the child, so that the quality of thinking in each case can be examined irrespective of whether the child's answer is 'right' or 'wrong'. It permits full exploration of the child's response to determine the course of subsequent questions. The aim is to follow the child's own thought in a way which is impossible by using standardised test procedures.

Piaget has shown that during the first 15 years of life, which include most of the years of statutory education, the child moves progressively through qualitatively different stages of thought, each of which is defined by a characteristic way of thinking. These stages are classified as sensorimotor, preoperational, concrete operational and formal operational. Each stage is characterised by a process of gradual development, beginning with an initial period of preparation and ending with a final period of achievement. Intellectual development does not proceed by a series of abrupt changes between one stage and the next. Furthermore the ages given for the various stages of development are averages. Some children pass through the different stages earlier whilst others do so later.

The sensorimotor stage lasts from birth to about 2 years. During this stage children explore their immediate environment using their vision and sense of touch. They begin to recognise that objects around them have an existence in their own right and are permanent. They can perceive themselves as objects among other objects. Their early thinking, however, is egocentric, that is, they find it difficult to see the world from any viewpoint other than their own.

The preoperational stage extends from the age of about 2 years to approximately 7 years. It may be subdivided into the preconceptual period (2 to 4 years) and the intuitive period (4 to 7 years). Each label indicates the characteristic mode of thinking which prevails during the period. It is difficult to treat these two periods exclusively from each other because intellectual development proceeds steadily and continuously during them.

During the preconceptual period, especially during the nursery school years, children begin to communicate through language and to represent objects symbolically by playing, drawing and later writing. Language develops rapidly but may be inadequate to convey what children are trying to express. Their use of words is inconsistent, indicating that they are not yet able to form true concepts. Thought is still immature and remains egocentric.

THE FOUNDATIONS OF GRAPHICACY

During the intuitive period, which broadly corresponds with the infant school years, children begin to form simple concepts. A concept may be defined as a class of objects or ideas normally represented by a word. Early concepts are very much influenced by the children's immediate environment and by stimuli that they personally experience. Thus children living in an urban area can describe houses correctly and distinguish them from shops. Children living in a rural area learn to describe cattle correctly and distinguish them from sheep. Language continues to develop swiftly during this period and may sometimes sound quite sophisticated. Thought is still dominated by immediate perceptions, however, and children can handle only one relationship at a time as they look at objects. Thus they can classify objects by shape or by colour, but not both simultaneously. Words such as 'big' and 'small' tend to be absolute rather than relative terms, their size depending on personal experience. Children's thinking during the infant school years is still mainly egocentric and events are all interpreted in relation to their own needs and actions.

The concrete operational stage is of crucial importance to the primary and middle school teacher since it covers the age range from 7 to 12 years. Concrete operational thinking constitutes the first true logical thought. Concrete operations are called 'concrete' because they relate directly to objects and not yet to verbally stated hypotheses. Concrete reasoning proceeds when the objects or the data which provide the basis for thought are physically present for children to handle. The idea of an 'operation' is a fundamental one in Piaget's theory of intellectual development. By this term is meant the way in which the mind absorbs all the facts presented to it and then digests this material and organises it into a framework or structure. The term operation thus refers to thinking which is internalised, that is, children begin to work things out 'in their heads'. As McNally (1973) has said, 'operational thinking is fundamentally the application of a logical system in the service of thought'.

Key ideas implicit in logical thinking are those of conservation and reversibility. During the stage of concrete operations children come to realise that the amount of liquid in a beaker remains the same when it is poured into another beaker with a different shape, or that a piece of plasticine retains its volume when its appearance is changed from that of a ball to an elongated sausage by rolling and stretching. The related process of reversibility indicates the ability to return mentally to the starting point. Thus the child understands that when the liquid is poured back into the original beaker it will show that it has retained its volume, and that when the plasticine is rolled back into a ball it will again show that volume has been conserved.

As they proceed through the stage of concrete operations primary school children learn to master several important concepts. Furthermore, they are not only able to form concepts but they realise that certain concepts include others. By looking at an atlas map of the British Isles, for example, they understand that the islands are divided into countries and that each country is further subdivided into counties. Related to this is the development of an understanding of the order of magnitude, which enables children to arrange objects according to size. Thus they appreciate that villages are smaller than towns, which in turn are smaller than cities. Children also appreciate symmetrical relationships and that lengths, areas and volumes are constant. They realise not only that the railway which connects London with Cardiff also connects Cardiff with London, but also that the distance is the same in both directions even if the time taken by an express train in one direction is shorter than that of a stopping train in the other direction. Another important concept developed by children who are reaching the end of the stage of concrete operations is that of reference systems. This requires the ability to use two or more criteria each arranged in series to locate a particular object. Thus they can learn to locate places on an atlas map by means of lines of latitude and longitude, or on an Ordnance Survey map by means of eastings and northings.

The formal operational stage is of great importance to the secondary school teacher since it covers the age range from 12 years onwards. It is the stage when children are finally released from the need to relate everything to their immediate environment or experience. They develop the ability to manipulate in their minds objects which are not physically present. They can thus begin to argue by assuming particular premises and working out their implications mentally. The fundamental difference in the approach of concrete and formal thinkers to the consideration of a problem can be summed up in the phrase 'the real versus the possible'. The formal thinker proceeds by considering all of the possible relations implied by the data and then attempting by logical analysis to make a judgment as to the truth or falsity of each possibility suggested.

This significant stage of development is characterised by three clearly identifiable modes of thinking (McNally, 1973). First, thinking is hypothetico-deductive in nature. The formal thinker proceeds by setting up hypotheses to be subsequently tested and either confirmed or refuted. In successively testing, confirming or refuting these hypotheses, the formal thinker is engaged in hypothetico-deductive reasoning. This is the procedure of scientific method and represents a distinct advance on concrete operations where the child only discovers relationships when they are linked to the immediate reality before him. Second, formal thinking is essentially proposition-al thinking. The formal thinker can follow the form of an argument independently of its concrete content and can man-ipulate the relationships which might exist, making prop-ositions about the data. It is this ability to follow the form of an argument whilst disregarding the content that gives this stage its label of formal operations. Third, formal thinking is combinatorial. This means that the formal thinker is able to isolate systematically all of the variables in a problem and to consider all the possible combinations. The variables are considered in turn and their effects either alone or in combination are examined.

To summarise, therefore, formal operational thinking is distinguished from concrete operational thinking because it is characterised by hypothesis testing, the ability to reason with propositions about the data and the isolation of all relevant variables and their possible combinations. These three characteristics are clearly interdependent in the process of formal reasoning. Hypotheses are set up on the basis of prop-ositions which take into account the respective variables.

The transition from concrete to formal operational thinking is an important one for the teacher to be able to detect. It takes place at widely differing times in individual children. Some investigators who have replicated Piaget's experiments believe that he was working mainly with children who were average to above average in ability. Thus Peel (1971) suggests that the transition takes place at the age of 13 years rather than 12 years in many children and there appear to be some who do not attain formal thinking until 14 or 15 years. Slow learning children may never achieve the stage of formal opera-tional thinking during their school lives. Even normal adults when faced with a novel, complex situation, may revert to concrete thinking until they have firmly grasped the various implications of the variables in a problem. The important point for the secondary school teacher is that most children in the first two years of the 11-16 or 11-18 comprehensive school will still be at the stage of concrete thinking. The transition to formal thinking will be a gradual one and its onset will vary widely among adolescents during the subsequent years of statutory education.

Topological Space

Space is itself a concept which is difficult to define. The nature of space has long been debated by psychologists and philosophers, whilst geographers use the concept in different contexts. 'Space in a room', 'space for building', 'space between towns' and 'territorial space' illustrate different uses of the word. Space is an idea in the mind which permits the structuring of relationships between objects. Space is subjective and relative, depending on the way it is structured by the mind on a particular occasion. There is no objective or absolute space; there are variations in the idea of space held by different people at different times. There are similarly considerable variations in the idea of space held by children at successive stages of their intellectual development.

Numerous experiments conducted over many years by Piaget and Inhelder (1956) and Piaget, Inhelder and Szeminska (1960) have shown that children's spatial understanding develops gradually and passes through three stages: topological, projective and Euclidean. The following account attempts to relate these three stages of spatial concept development to the stages of intellectual development described in the previous section. Spatial concept development takes place at two levels. It is confined to the perceptual level during the pre-school years, when children begin to understand their environment by exploring it. Development occurs at the con- ceptual level during the years of schooling, when children learn to represent their perceptions of the environment in the form of concepts.

Children's early understanding of their environment is entirely egocentric. During the sensorimotor stage (from birth to 2 years) they become aware of their spatial surroundings solely on a perceptual level. They perceive their immediate environment and explore it using their visual and tactile senses. Children learn from experience to distinguish between objects that are near to them and can be grasped, and those that are further away and beyond their reach. During the early part of the preoperational stage known as the preconceptual period (2-4 years) children start to develop an internal representation of space and are able to understand the locations of objects in relation to one another. They begin to move from purely perceptual understanding of their environment to initial spatial conception. This means that they become capable of representing their spatial perceptions mentally and of recalling these spatial images when they are not present for them to observe.

Children begin to develop a topological understanding of space during the later part of the preoperational stage known as the intuitive period (4-7 years). Infant school children learn to conceive of their environment in terms of objects which are connected to one another. The term 'topology' refers to the study of spatial equivalence, the most important prop- erty dealt with being that of proximity. This relationship can be stated only in terms of points which are connected to one another. The child starts by building up and using this elementary relationship of proximity and its related one of separation. Such relationships are termed topological by geometricians and are similarly regarded by them as elementary from the standpoint of the theoretical reconstruction of space.

When children understand simple connections between the parts of a whole they can soon learn to represent these connections on drawings in a very rough manner. A drawing is a representation, which means that the child is able to construct an image mentally. This is an ability which is much more advanced than that of mere perception itself. If children are asked to draw their route to school in a tray of damp sand or on paper they will simply show the connections between the places they know and remember, as is illustrated in Figure 1.1a. The viewpoint is highly egocentric and shows little understanding of such concepts as direction, orientation or distance. Nevertheless such a representation is an elementary map which is topological in structure. It consists simply of lines connecting points and does not show their correct positions or distances from one another.

Topological maps are used by adults when they serve the function of demonstrating connections between points. An adult may show a visitor the route from the town centre to his house by means of a drawing in which points represent major road junctions and lines represent the roads connecting them. A well known example of a topological map is the London Underground map which shows the location of stations as points and the track connecting them as straight or curved lines. British Rail inter-city services are shown on topological maps in a similar manner, as are suburban rail services in some conurbations.

Projective Space

Children's spatial understanding evolves from being topological to becoming projective during the stage of concrete operational thinking (7-12 years). The term 'projective' indicates the representation of three-dimensional objects such as buildings in two dimensions, either in elevation or in plan form. This ability emerges during the years of primary education, when children develop a greater awareness of the location of objects and of the relationships between them. It is closely related to the growth of the ability of children to put themselves into the position of other people and view objects from their point of view.

In one of their experiments Piaget and Inhelder (1956) demonstrate the gradual growth in children's appreciation of the relativity of perspectives in space. The child is shown a

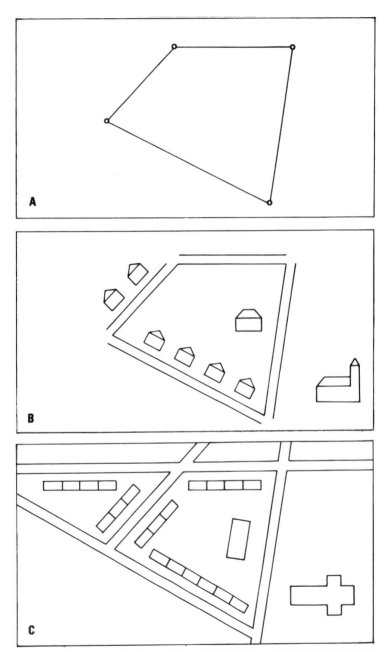

FIGURE 1.1. TOPOLOGICAL, PROJECTIVE AND EUCLIDEAN MAPS

one-metre square model of three mountains ranging in height
from 12 to 30 centimetres. This is placed in front of the
child so that the lowest mountain, coloured green and with a
little house on the summit, is in the right foreground. To
its left and slightly to the rear is a brown mountain, greater
in height and with a red cross on the summit. In the background stands the highest mountain, coloured grey and capped
with snow. A zigzag path descends the side of the green mountain and a rivulet runs down the side of the brown mountain.

The child sits in front of the model and a little wooden
doll is placed in various positions around the table on which
the model rests. The child's task is to discover what perspective the doll will see in each position. The child
remains stationary; only the doll moves. He has to try to
imagine and to reconstruct the changes in perspective that
accompany the doll's movements. Because the young child would
have difficulty in giving a verbal description, three
variations of the experiment are used. In one version the
child is asked to reproduce the view obtained by the doll at
different positions by arranging three pieces of cardboard,
shaped and coloured the same as each of the mountains. In a
second version he is shown a set of ten pictures taken from
different angles showing the mountains painted in the same
colours as the model and is asked to choose the picture which
shows what the doll would see. In another version he is asked
to choose a picture and then place the doll where it would have
to sit to see that view. All variations of the experiment give
similar results.

Children in the intuitive period (4-7 years) are incapable
of undertaking this kind of representative co-ordination of
perspectives. They imagine that the doll's view of the mountains is the same as their own. Children at this level are
very much tied to their own immediate perceptions. They are
unable to manipulate their own movements in thought and say,
for example, 'if I walked to the other side of the table I
should see that'. Nor are they able to manipulate the objects
that they see in thought, for example, 'the brown mountain on
the left would be on the right if the model were turned round'.
It has been argued by Donaldson (1978), however, that young
children are unable to perform the tasks in the three mountains
experiment because their use and understanding of language is
still developing. The situation does not make sense to them and
they do not fully understand what they are expected to do.
Young children are able to perform a simpler but comparable
task if they are carefully introduced to it in such a way that
they grasp what is being asked of them.

In the early part of the concrete operations stage at
about age 7 or 8 years children begin to realise the importance

of left-right and before-behind relationships which vary
according to the position of the observer. There are so many
of these relationships to be taken into account, however, that
even with only three mountains they are unable to deal with
all of them. They tend to sieze upon one particularly striking
feature that would be seen by the doll and look for it in the
pictures, apparently unaware of the other relationships between the mountains that have to be reconsidered. They are
able to make several correct arrangements of the pieces of
cardboard and some accurate judgments of the pictures, but
remain confused about others. They make considerable efforts
to do what is asked of them and they do manage to make a first
step away from their own position.

Later in the concrete operations stage at about age 9 or
10 years children manage to achieve complete relativity of
perspectives. They learn to co-ordinate all the relationships
and become capable of predicting correctly what the features
of the mountains and the relationships between them will be in
the various positions around the table. This experiment,
along with others on spatial concept development, brings out
repeatedly the difference between perceptual space and conceptual space, and the lag in development between the two.
There is little doubt that children in the intuitive period
do perceive or see the mountains as well as those at the concrete operations stage. What the younger children do not possess is the operational intelligence to co-ordinate the
relationships which are necessary for the formation of adequate
conceptions of space. It is not until about 9 or 10 years of
age that the majority of children are able to represent
clearly in their minds an all-round spatial construction.

The responses which children at the projective stage make
when asked to draw their route to school illustrate this
development. At age 7 to 8 years they produce picture maps
which show partial co-ordination and connection of places they
know well and there is some indication of orientation and
direction. Roads are shown correctly in plan form but buildings alongside them are frequently shown in side elevation,
as illustrated in Figure 1.1b. The shapes of buildings are
drawn so that they roughly resemble the real buildings that
they represent, and they are shown in approximately their
correct positions. Children's awareness of the objects around
them continues to be egocentric, however, so that buildings
that are important to them tend to be shown prominently and
those that are unimportant are omitted. As children reach the
age of 9 to 10 years their maps show more detail and better co-
ordination, and roads are correctly joined up to one another.
They show at least some buildings in plan form, and orientation
and direction are more accurate.

Some maps used by adults are drawn in projective form to
facilitate understanding. Examples are tourist maps of
historic towns which show the location of interesting buildings,
often drawn in elevation to assist their recognition, and the
means of reaching them. Some maps of upland landscapes popular
with visitors are drawn in semi-pictorial form, the perspective
being that of the artist sitting at a high viewpoint or that of
the camera taking an oblique photograph from a low-flying air-
craft.

Euclidean Space

The term 'Euclidean' refers to the spatial geometry of the mind
in which the relationships of objects in space are structured
in terms of horizontal and vertical lines, squares, rectangles,
triangles and circles. Important properties are those of open
space, as in a series of straight or curved lines, and closed
space, as in circles and squares. An understanding of
Euclidean space begins to take place towards the end of the
stage of concrete operational thinking, but most of it occurs
only after children have acquired the capacity for formal
operational thinking. Children's understanding of Euclidean
and projective properties certainly takes place long after
they understand topological relations.

In another experiment Piaget and Inhelder (1956) use a
model village containing such features as a few cottages, a
church and some trees, which are arranged on a base placed on
a table. The child is asked to draw these objects on a sheet
of paper smaller than the model, either as viewed directly
from above or as seen in oblique perspective. All the objects
thus have to be placed relative to one another at the same
time. The layout presents the child with the twofold problem,
that of seeing the village in a particular perspective, and
that of using Euclidean co-ordinates in transforming the
direct visual experience into a plan.

Children in the preconceptual period (2 to 4 years) are
unable to undertake this task. They achieve neither spatial
nor one-to-one correspondence between the two layouts. Thus
they may draw fewer or more objects than are actually used in
the model. Those they do draw are not placed in corresponding
positions on the layout. The objects may be bunched up together or strung out in a line.

During the intuitive period (4 to 7 years) children choose
objects in the model and try to draw them in similar positions
on their paper. Nevertheless they do not locate a particular
position according to any system of reference. There is still
no co-ordination between the arrangement of objects in relation
to one another and to the edges of the paper on which they are

11

drawn. Thus a group of objects may be crowded together on one side of the paper whilst other objects are placed without regard to the position occupied on the model. Towards the age of 7 years children may establish certain sets of relations in an intuitive way.

During the stage of concrete operational thought (7 to 12 years) children gradually build up a system of reference. They begin to arrange objects according to the two dimensions of the model and corresponding to a particular viewpoint. Between the ages of 7 and 10 children learn to arrange the objects in their drawings by taking account of left-right and before-behind relations, the top of the drawing representing the background. Although errors of detail still persist, especially with regard to depth, these drawings are genuine two-dimensional representations. Moreover, from the moment they start to draw, children relate the various objects to the edge of the model and distribute them according to the size of the paper, in the same way that they are arranged on the model. The new and significant development shown by children in the 7 to 10 age group is that they relate the objects to the edge of the paper whilst at the same time arranging them with reference to one another in two dimensions. Conceptual relationships are understood and this indicates the attainment of a system of co-ordinates. At the same time as this organisation of Euclidean space becomes apparent, there is a distinct improvement in the treatment of perspective. The overhead view is distinguished from the oblique perspective, but drawings illustrate every stage of development, ranging from roofs shown in side elevation to others shown from above with the ridge running down the centre.

Nevertheless some deficiencies remain until children approach 10 years of age. They do not gauge distances with any degree of accuracy, although they try to do so. Whilst distances from left to right are rendered fairly accurately, distances in depth, shown vertically in the drawing, are considerably underestimated. In the case of the oblique view such distortion might be attributed to lack of appreciation of perspective applied to distance, but the error also occurs in the plan view. Furthermore, when children try to reduce their plans to scale, they leave the sizes of objects unchanged, merely placing them closer together.

Children begin to master distance and proportion after about the age of 10 years. There is a more careful and accurate judgment of distance and an important advance in reducing drawings to scale. Whilst children under 10 simply push objects together without reducing their size, those over 10 reduce the size of the objects as well as the distances

between them. Children are now mastering the task of
drawing the layout by taking into account not only position
and distance, using a system of co-ordinates, but also perspective and proportion. All that children still have to acc-
omplish is the production of a purely schematic plan. Instead
of a drawing of material objects placed in front of them they
have to learn to produce a diagram of the layout in which the
positions of the objects are established accurately by measurement. This is achieved by children when they reach the stage
of formal operations. Only at this stage is the concept of a
diagrammatic layout acquired in a broad and general way,
complete with accurate measurement of distance and proportional reduction to scale in addition to the understanding of
relations between objects.

It is precisely the development of formal operational
thought involving abstract reasoning that enables children to
understand maps and co-ordinate axes in their school work.
Hence children aged 11 to 12 years tend to display a combination of individually worked out and formally learned concepts.
The understanding of Euclidean space requires an accurate
conception of the spatial relationships between places. Most
children are now able to draw true maps which are detailed
and co-ordinated. Direction, orientation, distance and scale
are all shown with reasonable accuracy. Maps are drawn properly in plan form and buildings are no longer shown in side
elevation. Symbols are used to indicate important features so
that a legend to the map becomes necessary. Children rarely
achieve the kind of map drawing ability illustrated in Figure
1.1c until they reach the beginning of formal operational
thought.

During adolescence spatial understanding continues to
mature and with it develops the ability to study maps and draw
conclusions about spatial location, distributions and relationships. This kind of understanding and reasoning is needed for
reading and interpreting Ordnance Survey maps, a skill which is
required in public examinations in geography at age 16. The
ability to use hypothetico-deductive reasoning is also needed
in undertaking field study investigations which may be submitted for assessment as part of these examinations. Adolescents at the stage of formal operational thought are not
only able to use the hypothetico-deductive procedures of
science and mathematics but also are capable of adopting the
role of would-be social reformers. Their ability to theorise
and criticise enables them to see that the way the world is
run is only one of many possible ways in which it could be run.
They can conceive of alternative ways in which it might be run
better. In other words, adolescents at this stage think about
other possibilities that they see in the world around them and

also hypothesise about what they imagine might be true. They can think in the abstract.

This outline of Piaget's theory of intellectual development and its relationship to the development of spatial concepts has stressed the sequential nature of learning. Children have to understand certain fundamental experiences before they can understand more complex ones. This implies that such experiences need to be carefully graded, although other factors such as maturation, or natural physical growth, and the children's general view of the world as they see it in their surrounding environment, also determine their depth of understanding. The change from one stage of development to the next is transitional and each stage involves a period of formation and attainment before it is complete. Although the ages of attainment may vary considerably among children, the order of succession of the stages is constant. Thus children have to pass through the preoperational stage before they can attain the concrete operational stage, and they cannot reach the formal operational stage before they have passed through the concrete operational stage. Furthermore, development is a linear or 'end on' process in so far as something that has been understood by a child at an earlier stage is incorporated into his way of thinking at a later stage. In other words, the child does not just adopt a more advanced way of thinking and discard the earlier one altogether. Instead he modifies the earlier way of thinking and incorporates it into his new interpretation.

The development of spatial concepts in children as identified by Piaget has been linked by Catling (1978a) to the development of their understanding of three fundamental concepts in geography: spatial location, spatial distribution and spatial relationship. At the perceptual level of development children first show an awareness of the spatial location of objects in the environment around them. This subsequently develops into a recognition of the spatial distribution of objects in their environment. Finally children appreciate the existence of spatial relationships between the various objects. A similar sequence may be observed at the conceptual level of development. At the topological stage children understand spatial location solely in terms of points connected to them in a simple linear manner. When children manage to move away from this egocentric viewpoint and adopt a projective one, they are able to relate various objects to each other and understand the structure of their spatial distribution. By the time they reach the Euclidean stage of spatial concept development they are able to co-ordinate locations using abstract reference systems and comprehend the relationships between objects.

THE FOUNDATIONS OF GRAPHICACY

The relationship between Piaget's stages of intellectual development and the pupils' understanding of geographical concepts has been discussed by Graves (1975). He points out that growth in understanding of higher level concepts in geography is likely to be a slow process in many pupils, being dependent upon mental maturation and the acquisition of sophisticated language. He regards Piaget's theory as a useful tool because it helps the teacher to appreciate how views of the environment held by children and adolescents change as they grow older. It ·is important for the teacher to be aware of the concepts and perceptions of pupils at different ages and to understand the kinds of mental operations they are capable of performing at various stages.

Although Piaget did not set out to contribute directly to educational practice, his extensive studies of children's thinking led him to acquire firm convictions about the ways in which children should be taught. Piaget (1971) made it clear that he viewed with disfavour what he called 'the traditional school' and strongly supported what he called 'the new methods of education'. The traditional school imposed certain constraints upon children and used receptive methods of learning, whereas the new methods encouraged the positive involvement of children and used active methods of learning. Piaget consistently maintained this position in the course of his work. McNally (1973) concludes that Piaget's chief contribution to educational practice is in the field of method as it is applied to school curricula. Whilst Piaget was interested to some extent with what is taught, he was much more concerned with how it is taught. It is with methods of teaching that the present book is mainly concerned, and the methods advocated are under-pinned by Piaget's theory of intellectual and spatial concept development.

2 Some Problems of Graphicacy

As the pupils' understanding of spatial concepts develops, so
does their ability to comprehend the representation of these
concepts on spatial documents. The communication of spatial
concepts requires certain levels of competence in literacy,
numeracy and graphicacy. Maps and photographs are the spatial
documents which are most widely used in school geography and
environmental studies courses. Both of these documents, however, present numerous perceptual and conceptual problems for
children. It is essential that the teacher should be aware of
these problems as they occur at all stages of children's
development. They are discussed in this chapter in the light
of the nature of maps and in particular their function as a
means of communicating information. Problems encountered by
children of various ages in reading and interpreting large
scale and small scale maps are illustrated by reference to
some studies which have been undertaken in Britain, Australia
and the United States. The interpretation of vertical and
oblique aerial photographs by children is subsequently considered.

The Nature of Maps

Most people use maps either as a means of finding the location
of a place or as a means of getting to a place. For these
purposes a large scale street map, such as the A to Z road map
or Geographia town map, may be used to find a route from one
place to another in a town and reference to the scale enables
the distance between them to be measured. A smaller scale road
map of a region or country shows the routes between towns and
distances may be given between points or major routes. Location, direction and distance are the main everyday uses of maps.

Some maps may also be used for the purposes of discovering
the main features or characteristics of an area. The popular
Ordnance Survey maps show not only location and routes but

also relief and certain other aspects of the landscape such as
woodland, and useful information for visitors, such as car
parks. In rural areas walkers using footpaths can relate them
to relief features shown on the maps. The reading and interpretation of these maps are skills which form part of courses
leading to public examinations.

A specialised function of maps is that of storing and
displaying information. Maps which are compiled for specific
purposes are known as thematic. Examples are television and
newspaper weather maps and planning maps produced by regional
and local planning authorities. Others are land utilisation
maps showing the urban and rural use of land, and maps of the
density of population in various parts of a country, both of
which assist the perception and understanding of geographical
relationships. Inferences can sometimes be drawn from a
systematic analysis of the spatially distributed data contained
in such maps.

Maps show data by means of words, numbers and symbols.
Words are used to name places and important features on maps.
Numbers are used to show distances and heights as well as to
identify grid lines or lines of latitude and longitude.
Symbols take the form of points, such as those indicating
churches, railway stations and other buildings; lines, such as
roads, railways, rivers and contours; and area symbols, such
as the shaded area representing the land occupied by buildings
in a town, or the land covered with woodland in a rural area.
It will be apparent that this combination of words, numbers
and symbols makes the map a complex document.

A map is a scaled abstraction of reality. It is a
representation of selected phenomena on a part of the earth's
surface. Any definition of a map must be based on its
essential quality of being a representation of objects in
space. The difficulty of defining space has already been
discussed and is further complicated as far as a map is concerned because the map itself occupies space. Yet the space
represented on it is a scaled down version of reality. Space
shown on a map normally refers to 'place', 'area', 'region'
or 'environment'. The term 'place' refers simply to an
undefined portion of space. 'Area' is a mathematical concept
which is often used in geography to refer to space of widely
differing orders of magnitude. 'Region' is likewise a term
frequently employed in geography to refer to large amounts of
space on the earth's surface. The word 'environment' is sometimes used to refer to ecological relationships which are not
necessarily spatial. For these reasons two American experts
in the field of cartography, Robinson and Petchenik (1976),
prefer to define a map as 'a graphic representation of the
milieu'.

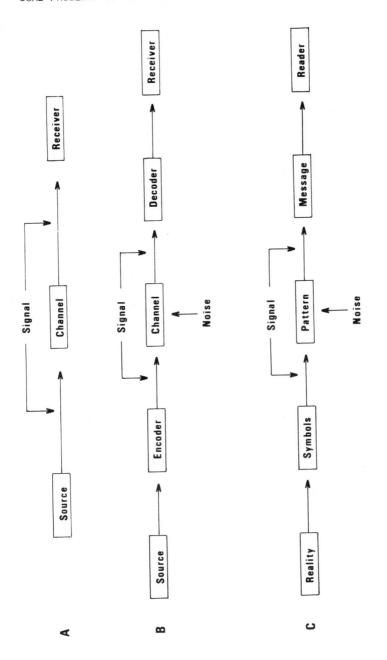

FIGURE 2.1. THE MAP AS A COMMUNICATION SYSTEM

SOME PROBLEMS OF GRAPHICACY

An essential feature of a map is that it is a means of communication. Just as most writing assumes that someone will read it, so most map making assumes that someone will look at the map. The author-reader and map maker-map reader transfer are both systems of communication. At the simplest level a typical communications network consists of a source which transmits the information, a channel which conveys the message and a receiver at the other end (Figure 2.1a). To take an everyday example, a television studio would be the source, the air which carries the sound and picture would be the channel, and the viewer looking at his television set would be the receiver. If examined in more detail, however, the basic system will include the recognition of an encoder between the source and the channel, and a decoder between the channel and the receiver (Figure 2.1b). The purpose of the encoder is to improve the efficiency of the communication. In the television analogy, the voice of the presenter constitutes an encoder which takes the main points from the source and transforms them into sound waves. The ears of the viewer constitute a decoder which transforms the sound waves back into the main points. An apparently inevitable component of every communication system, however, is an element termed 'noise' which interferes with the channel or signal. Examples are inaudible voice sounds in speech and distortions of the picture in television. In the generalised communication system the noise is shown as entering at the channel or signal stage (Figure 2.1b).

The process of communication through maps broadly resembles the generalised communication system. The source is the real world, and the encoder is the mind of the map maker who employs a large number of symbols on the map to indicate the presence of a wide variety of features – points, lines and areas. The channel or signal is the graphic pattern provided by these points, lines and areas on a sheet of paper. The decoder is the mind of the map reader who is the receiver of the information. It is in the process of decoding that the receiver attempts to make some sense of the complex patterns before his eyes. The noise is the distracting information which interferes with his attempts to focus upon the task in hand, such as that of deciding on the best route between two places on a map (Figure 2.1c).

The generalised model of a communication system simply assumes a message, its transmission and its receipt. A specialist system such as the communication of information through maps, however, involves complicated processes of selection in both the encoding by the map maker and in the decoding by the map reader. These processes, together with the inevitable interference from noise, results in a discrepancy between the real world on the one hand and the image

visualised by the map reader on the other hand. This discrepancy is due partly to the highly personal and individual
images of reality held by both the map maker and the map
reader, and partly to the methods used in coding the message
to convert reality into a map and in decoding the message to
convert the map back to reality.

The process of decoding by the map reader has two components. First, he has to be able to identify the symbols on
a map by their appearance; for example, he has to know that a
square or circle surmounted by a cross can be labelled as a
church with a tower or a spire. Second, the map reader has to
be able to comprehend the concept that the symbol represents
in reality; for example, he has to understand that the square
or circle surmounted by a cross is an abstract representation
of a feature which he would recognise in the real world as a
church with a tower or a spire. It will be clear that the
second component, comprehension, is more complex than the
first one, identification. The processes of identification
and comprehension develop slowly in children throughout the
stage of concrete thinking. By the time they have begun to
think abstractly they are able to comprehend the meaning of a
wide range of abstract map symbols.

Children who have difficulty in reading a map are
experiencing problems in decoding the messages transmitted by
the map maker. The process of communication suffers from
interference and the messages are misinterpreted. Hence
pupils who have difficulty in reading maps are experiencing
large amounts of map user noise. They are seeing the various
aspects of a map in ways which are different from those of the
map maker. If the noise is excessive the process of map
communication becomes unproductive and ineffective.

In view of the widespread use of the map as a means of
communication it is surprising that so little is known about
the process. Two American experts in the field of cartography
have concluded that there has not been 'a thorough delineation
of the methodological and philosophical bases on which an
analysis of the acquisition and transmission of spatial knowledge via the map could be conducted' (Robinson and Petchenik,
1976). The same authors believe that the nature of the map
as an image and the manner in which it functions as a mode of
communication between map maker and map reader deserve much
deeper consideration than they have so far received. Such
consideration entails more than an analysis of the physical
characteristics of the map as a document. They stress that
'the emphasis must shift from the map as a static graphic
display to the cognitive and perceptual activities of the individuals who interact with maps'. Piaget and his co-workers

in Switzerland have made valuable contributions to understanding the child's conception of space. Several investigations carried out in Britain, Australia and the United States have examined ways in which pupils of different ages handle maps and some of these studies will now be considered.

Large Scale Maps

An analysis of young children's understanding of a map and some of the underlying mapping concepts has been carried out in Australia by Gerber (1981a). He studied 80 children aged 6 to 8 years in Brisbane primary schools. The children's understanding of a plan view was tested by asking them to represent on a sheet of paper four separate objects in the classroom and then their school building. He found that most children could draw plan views of objects which have simple geometrical shapes but not more complex ones. When he asked the children to draw a cluster of objects in the classroom, he found that a majority of children were unable to represent the observed arrangement accurately. He noted the considerable difficulty that the children experienced in arranging simple clusters of phenomena, a finding that agrees with that of Piaget. He suggested that teachers should not expect young children to observe simple map forms and the spatial arrangement of objects. Gerber also found that whilst children could estimate short distances in the classroom when they can see a metre rule nearby, their judgement of longer visible distances (over 100 metres) was haphazard and erroneous. He noted that children need plenty of practice in measuring short and long distances around their school so that they can begin to appreciate distance.

The way in which children develop an understanding of the concept of direction was also illuminated by Gerber's study. The sequence of development is more complicated than that of seeing objects in front of or behind other objects, to the right or left of other objects, and north or south of particular points. He found a much more extensive sequence of development which included such responses as near or next to, far or far away, a verbal statement or a sign without indicated direction. Gerber's study shows that before children learn how to use the cardinal points of the compass they use a variety of substitutes for direction, and that after some instruction young children can handle a compass and develop a rudimentary understanding of the cardinal points.

Gerber's findings support the assumption that young children reach higher levels of achievement when the distinct elements of a map are taught separately. It appears that young children cannot deal with whole maps but can manage to handle different elements one at a time. It is also important that children's encounters with maps are presented as concrete learning experiences using the immediate environment. A similar conclusion was reached in another study of eleven-year-old children by Gerber and Wilson (1979) which suggested that children should experience concrete reference systems in the school grounds before they are introduced to abstract reference systems.

Basic concepts in map understanding are those of symbolism, scale, direction and location. Tests to assess comprehension of these concepts were administered to 105 children aged 8 to 13 in a primary and a middle school in Leeds by Charlton (1975). She found that whilst the understanding of all four map concepts improved with age, it was particularly noticeable that definite stages could be detected in the children's understanding of scale and location. Both of these concepts involve Euclidean notions and, once they had been understood, the children seemed to be able to apply a similar level of understanding to most maps. The other two concepts, symbolism and direction, appeared to be much more dependent upon instruction. Symbolism, involving the ability to understand the reality behind a map using a particular set of symbols, was more readily grasped with a large scale maps of the home area than with small scale maps of more distant areas. Charlton concluded that map work with younger pupils should be based on large scale maps of the local area where the map can be studied in conjunction with the real environment. When children are able to appreciate the conventions on large scale maps they are more likely to understand those on smaller scale maps.

When basic map skills among 140 pupils aged 11 to 12 in the first year of a mixed comprehensive school near Sheffield were studied by Salt (1971) direction and scale were found to be the two skills that were least well developed when pupils entered the secondary school. Direction was still a problem at the end of the first year of secondary education, reversals being one source of error, especially among pupils in the lower range of ability. Salt recommended more systematic teaching which aims at developing the concept of direction rather than the ability merely to write it down on paper when the north point is given. Salt also found that most pupils could handle scale correctly when it simply involved computation, but when they had to compare scales the majority did not appear to have acquired a true understanding of the concept. He suggested that the teaching of scale would seem to be appropriate at about the age of 12 for most pupils, a conclusion that agrees with that of Piaget and Inhelder (1956) who showed that an understanding of proportion depends on the attainment of formal operational thinking. Salt's observation of the difficulties encountered by pupils in drawing plans

also support the contention of Piaget and Inhelder that comprehension of an abstract plan requires formal operational
thought and that a true understanding of maps is not achieved
until the spatial concepts needed for abstract plan drawing
have been acquired.

The ability to generalise from a distribution on a map
and to compare two separate distributions was investigated by
Heamon (1973). He tested in several ways 80 children between
the ages of 8 and 14 in Abingdon and district. For example,
they were shown a 1:10,560 (6 inches to one mile) map containing several villages, the houses of which were coloured
red, situated in a discontinuous belt running from west-north-
west to east-south-east. Rivers were coloured blue, land over
200 feet brown, and woods were shown by green dots. The
children were given a piece of paper with the shape of the
map frame already drawn and asked to draw one shape to show
where most of the houses were. Pupils aged 14 years were
better able to draw the outline of the built-up area than the
younger children. In a subsequent test using the same map the
pupils were asked what they noticed about the position of
nearly all the woods. Heamon found that by the age of 12
about half the children were capable of perceiving a relationship between the two generalised distributions and that this
ability had been acquired by nearly all of them by the age of
14. Heamon's tests were devised to examine Piaget's idea of
'centration', the tendency for children to focus their attention on a limited number of stimuli. Piaget observed that
this tendency decreased as children grew older and this is
illustrated by the tendency of younger children to look for
micro-features rather than macro-features on a map.

Topographical maps showing relief are more difficult to
understand because of the complex array of features which
they contain. Some of the problems encountered by older
pupils in reading and interpreting these maps have been investigated by Boardman and Towner (1979). They devised a
test covering a range of map reading skills and administered
it to a total of 578 fifth form pupils in their final year of
statutory education (age 15-16) in twelve Birmingham schools.
The pupils were divided into three groups: those who were
following O-level courses in geography (209 pupils), those
following CSE mode 1 courses (203 pupils) and those following
CSE mode 3 courses based on the Geography for the Young School
Leaver (GYSL) project (166 pupils).

One of the four sections of the test was concerned with
the pupils' understanding of relief. It dealt with the
visualisation of a three-dimensional landscape from a two-
dimensional map and included questions on the height of the

23

land and its slope. The pupils were provided with a contour
sketch map of part of a 1:50,000 Ordnance Survey map of an
area 8km by 5km to the north-east of Birmingham (Figure 2.2).
They were asked to shade in pencil on the sketch map the area
which was below 91 metres in height. The maximum number of
marks allocated to this question was three and the percentages
of pupils who obtained 3, 2, 1 and 0 marks are shown in the
first four lines of Table 2.1.

It will be seen that whilst 80 per cent of the O-level
pupils performed this apparently straightforward task with
complete accuracy, only 43 per cent of the CSE pupils and 17
per cent of the GYSL pupils did so. The overall scores for
all pupils show that just under half (49 per cent) obtained
full marks, nearly a quarter (24 per cent) two marks and the
remaining quarter one mark or none at all. The marking scheme
is shown in Figure 2.3 and the errors made by pupils deserve
study. Some pupils stopped shading when they reached the 76m
contour (Figure 2.3c, f). Apparently these pupils did not
realise that land below 76m was also below 91m. Some also
failed to shade land below 61m (Figure 2.3b, c, e). Other pupils
started their shading at the 76m contour (Figure 2.3b, d).
They appear to have chosen the nearest contour bearing a number
less than 91m, indicating that they failed to appreciate the
continuous fall in the height of the land between one contour
and the next. A few pupils shaded land between 91 and 76m,
left unshaded land between 76m and 61m, and then shaded land
below 61m (Figure 2.3f). All of these errors indicate that
half of the pupils had an incomplete understanding of what a
contour map represents.

A further question asked the pupils to look at each of the
four short lines A, B, C and D in turn, decide which end was
higher and draw a circle round that end. The results are
shown in Table 2.1. On average 92 per cent of the O-level
pupils, 81 per cent of the CSE pupils and 61 per cent of the
GYSL pupils obtained correct answers for these four short lines.
Slightly more pupils circled the wrong end of line D than A,
B or C, possibly because D was parallel to the contour and
pupils had to appreciate the slope of the valley. The next
question which asked pupils to decide which of the four lines
lay on the steepest slope, however, was answered wrongly by
more pupils in all groups. 77 per cent of the O-level pupils
correctly selected line B, but only 49 per cent of CSE pupils
and 31 per cent of the GYSL pupils did so. Pupils who gave
incorrect answers did not appreciate the relationship between
closeness of contours and steepness of slope. Finally, the
pupils were asked to estimate the height of the land at the
points E, F and G on the sketch map. Point E was the easiest
to determine because it lay on a contour. Point F, however,

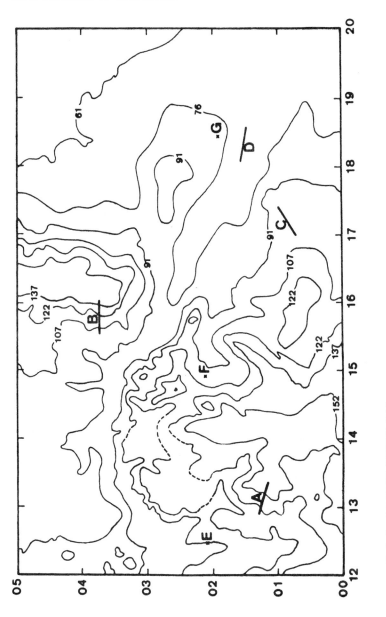

FIGURE 2.2. CONTOUR SKETCH MAP

25

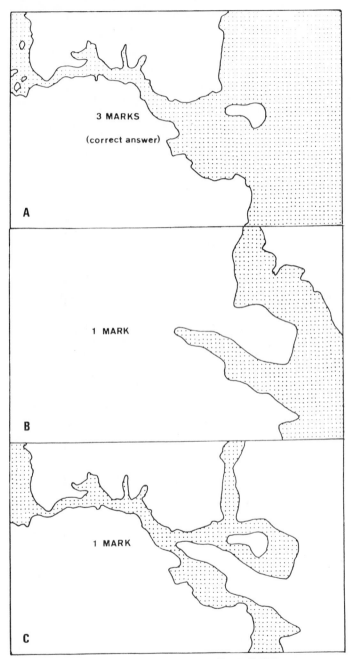

FIGURE 2.3. PUPILS' SHADING OF CONTOUR SKETCH MAP

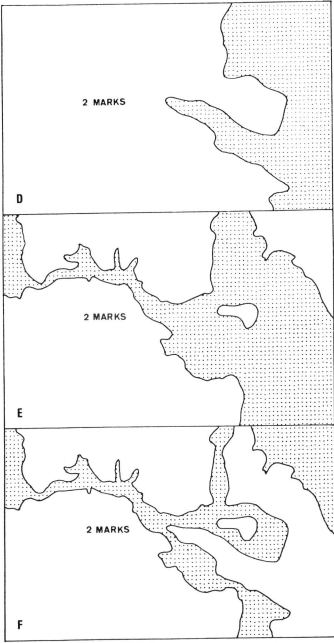

FIGURE 2.3. (Continued)   Source: Boardman and Towner (1979)

TABLE 2.1 SCORES ON RELIEF SHADING AND HEIGHT ESTIMATION

	O-LEVEL			CSE			GYSL			TOTAL		
	BOYS n=118 %	GIRLS n=91 %	TOTAL n=209 %	BOYS n=120 %	GIRLS n=83 %	TOTAL n=203 %	BOYS n=106 %	GIRLS n=60 %	TOTAL n=166 %	BOYS n=344 %	GIRLS n=234 %	TOTAL n=578 %
RELIEF 3	86	72	80	51	32	43	22	10	17	54	42	49
RELIEF 2·	11	22	15	22	39	29	27	27	28	20	29	24
RELIEF 1	1	4	3	17	17	17	23	38	28	13	17	15
RELIEF 0	2	2	2	10	12	11	28	25	27	13	12	12
LINE A	96	83	90	77	75	76	57	50	54	77	72	75
LINE B	97	93	96	90	87	89	68	62	66	86	83	85
LINE C	96	96	96	87	84	86	56	57	56	80	82	81
LINE D	85	90	87	75	70	73	69	70	70	76	78	77
STEEPEST	79	74	77	52	43	49	33	27	31	55	51	54
POINT E	91	86	89	64	60	63	48	23	39	69	61	65
POINT F	77	57	68	33	23	29	18	13	16	44	34	40
POINT G	86	81	84	62	49	57	38	20	31	63	54	59

Source: Boardman and Towner (1979)

proved to be much more difficult because it lay midway between two contours and was estimated correctly to within two metres by 68 per cent of the O-level pupils but only 29 per cent of the CSE pupils and 16 per cent of the GYSL pupils. Rather more managed to estimate the height of point G because it lay near a numbered contour.

Erroneous ideas about relief as shown by contours were also revealed in another study, on this occasion involving 166 first form pupils (age 11-12) and 170 third form pupils (age 13-14) in six schools in the West Midlands (Boardman, 1982a). Pupils in both age groups were asked to shade all land above 91 metres on a much simpler contour sketch map. Similar mistakes to those in the earlier study were made. Errors occurred not only in shading the land but also in marking the higher end of each of three short lines and in estimating the height of three given points. The scores of first form pupils were lower than those of third form pupils, and this, together with the results of the earlier study with fifth form pupils, suggests that understanding of relief as shown on contour maps develops steadily with age as pupils enter the stage of formal operational thinking but is still incomplete in many pupils by the time they leave school.

Inability to visualise the solid reality from the contours on maps was also noted by Satterly (1964) in a study of 60 fourth form secondary school pupils in Bristol. Many pupils aged 14 to 15 who could recognise the contour representation of landforms when these were discrete had difficulty in identifying these same landforms when they were part of the more confusing contour organisation on a map. Satterly's study is of interest because he attempted to discover whether performance in map reading could be associated with certain psychological variables. He gave the pupils a battery of psychological tests for ability in spatial concepts, spatial skill and spatial perception alongside a series of tests of mapwork performance. The scores on the two sets of tests revealed a statistically strong and significant correlation between the psychological variables measured and performance in mapwork. Pupils who obtained high scores in tests of spatial ability tended to obtain high scores in tests of mapwork. Satterly then analysed his data further to find out whether any particular psychological test could best predict performance in mapwork. The analysis indicated that the best single predictor of mapwork ability was provided by performance in the test of the perception of embedded shapes. This suggests that pupils who are able to discriminate between similar shapes, such as the contour patterns for different kinds of valley, are likely to perform well in mapwork tests.

A topographical map contains a mass of embedded shapes which the pupil has to attempt to disentangle in order to make sense of the information provided by the map. Satterly recommended that, in order to improve performance in mapwork, teaching programmes should be devised to increase perceptual skills and improve spatial concept development. He suggested that perceptual skills might be increased if children are provided with more experiences involving the analysis of shape, as in art lessons, the children being encouraged to talk about the process and thus become more conscious of it. The level of spatial concept might be developed by means of experiences in which the attention of pupils is focused on the spatial arrangement of objects within three dimensions and of their own position in relation to them, as in drawing and model making. Again the pupils should be encouraged to note and verbally communicate the changes in position, apparent size and shape of objects that occur with changes of viewpoint.

The design of maps and the attributes of the pupils may affect their understanding of maps and ability to use them. Gerber (1981b) identified three aspects of map design and ten attributes of the map user, and investigated their influence on competence in map language (understanding of maps) and performance in map language (ability to use maps) in pupils at the concrete level of map reasoning. The aspects of map design were colour in map signs, map generalisation, and map lettering. The attributes of the map user were age, map reading ability, home environment, previous experience with maps, understanding the concept of a map, drawing ability, attitude to maps, verbal and non-verbal reasoning and spatial ability. A total of 640 children aged 8 to 14 years in upper primary and lower secondary classes in Brisbane schools were tested and multivariate analysis was performed on the test results. Of the three aspects of map design, map generalisation and map lettering were found to be significant influences on the pupils' map reasoning level and their competence and performance in map language. Colour in map signs influenced competence and performance. As far as the attributes of the map user were concerned, map reading ability and verbal and non-verbal reasoning ability were found to influence map reasoning level and competence and performance in map language. Age, home environment and drawing ability influenced map reasoning level and competence in map language. Previous experience with maps, understanding the concept of a map, and spatial ability influenced competence and performance. These complex interrelationships indicate the wide range of matters which can affect ability to read and use maps.

There is some evidence that boys tend to do better than girls in operations involving spatial ability. The difference appears to be small in younger children but gradually widens as they grow older. Macfarlane-Smith (1964) observed that spatial ability develops more quickly in boys than in girls and becomes noticeable in the years of secondary education. Charlton (1975) in her study of symbolism, scale, direction and location with children aged 8 to 13 found no significant difference between boys and girls in understanding the four concepts. Salt (1971) found that girls aged 11 to 12 were as competent as boys of the same age on tests involving large scale maps, but that boys were better than girls on map tests involving locational knowledge of their environment and the British Isles. Boys also obtained higher scores on the spatial concepts tests which Salt administered. Boys consistently obtained higher scores than girls in all sections of the map test administered to more than 500 pupils aged 15 to 16 by Boardman and Towner (1979). Similarly Sandford (1970) found that boys had significantly higher scores than girls in a study of atlas maps involving 1,600 pupils aged 11 to 15 which will be considered in the next section.

Small Scale Maps

Atlas maps present considerable perceptual problems for children because they involve translating information about large areas from the symbolic form in which they appear on small scale maps into a meaningful conceptual form. A detailed account of the difficulties encountered by pupils aged 10 to 15 years when using atlas maps has been given in an American study by Bartz (1965). She gave short informal oral tests on a series of atlas maps. She found that pupils understood what direction means and were familiar with the four cardinal points but uncertain about the intermediate points. Although the convention is to place north at the top of a map, the pupils became confused when the north point was missing. The pupils were also not immediately aware of the concept of scale. Even when a linear scale was given on a map younger pupils often did not refer to it. By the age of 12 or 13 years pupils referred to the scale line for measuring simple distances. Most pupils had not developed any systematic procedure for using a linear scale, and scale expressed as a representative fraction was not understood at all. Bartz found that the only symbols which pupils fully understood were a black dot representing a town or city, a star representing a capital city, a wavy blue line representing a river and a blue area representing a lake or an ocean. The pupils experienced considerable difficulty in attempting to identify countries solely by means of lines drawn around them. It was much easier for them to identify countries on the basis of colour changes. The pupils had an inadequate understanding

31

of the terminology of political units so that they made errors
in distinguishing the concept of a country from that of a
continent.

Other difficulties gave rise to incorrect concepts of the
nature of maps and of the world. They were largely associated
with errors in perceiving information presented in atlas maps.
The children perceived symbols but did not fully understand
them, and did not refer to the legend for an explanation of
the meaning of colours, they made mistakes in reading and
interpreting what was shown on the maps. Instead of referring
to the key to coloured tints showing altitude, for example,
children frequently used some other association they had
previously learnt, thus equating green with grass and brown
with desert. Bartz observed the general tendency of children
to interpret the atlas map too literally. She also noted that
they were often unable to distinguish between different styles
and sizes of type face and concluded that the most important
symbols on the atlas map were those that formed the lettering.
Pupils were more conscious of the names on a map than they
were of any other element. Their understanding of much of the
other symbolism on the map depended upon how readily the names
were seen and understood. Bartz (1970) has undertaken some
detailed studies of the legibility of maps and has emphasised
the importance of clarity and simplicity in the presentation
of information to pupils. She observes that few published
maps for classroom use are truly simple, making one point in
a clear manner. Instead most maps try to make many points,
and often do not succeed in making any one point clearly.
Maps which are too detailed are liable to be misread because
the significant information which is being sought from them
is easily lost in a mass of other data.

Some illuminating work on pupils' perceptions of atlas
maps has been carried out in England by Sandford (1967, 1970,
1972). He first examined the perception of a general or
politico-relief map of Asia by 340 boys and girls in a grammar school in a London Borough (Sandford, 1967). They were
asked to write down in 20 minutes what the map told them about
the continent. Their answers were analysed and this unguided
search of an atlas map indicated that the pupils appeared to
scan the map in a variety of ways. Pupils often began somewhere near the centre of the map and moved from left to right
(west to east) as in reading a book; sometimes they moved in a
clockwise direction around the coastline; and occasionally
they moved from top to bottom (north to south). The general
tendency to read the map like a book, from north-west to south-
east, could hardly be regarded as the most appropriate scanning
strategy in visual search. Boldness of type, familiarity with
a particular name on the map, interest, frequency and pattern
all influenced the pupils' choice of symbols to record in

their answers.

In his second study Sandford (1970, 1972) constructed a test to measure the ability of pupils to form realistic concepts of the world when using atlas maps. The test consisted of a battery of three interpretative test exercises each comprising eight multiple-choice questions about an atlas map: a political map of the world, a relief map of Africa and a pair of thematic maps of Australasia, one of annual rainfall and the other of natural vegetation. The test was administered to a stratified cluster sample of 1,600 boys and girls studying geography in the first four years of secondary education in 21 schools in London and the Home Counties. These were divided into pupils taking O-level, CSE and non-examination courses. The test was the easiest that twelve experienced geography teachers could devise, yet the mean score was as low as 10 out of 24. Less than one per cent of the pupils answered 75 per cent of the items correctly.

Many pupils experienced perceptual difficulties and seemed unable to grasp basic concepts or use elementary techniques. Pupils of all ages displayed a low level of map realism. Errors made by the pupils were often due to their failure to appreciate standards of size and length and to realise the limitations of the small scale map. Thus 42 per cent of the pupils thought that because the map showed only three towns in New Zealand, there were only three towns; 53 per cent thought that because the map did not show any railway stations between Bombay and Madras, there were no stations; 31 per cent could not give the straight-line distance from the Cape of Good Hope to Victoria Falls. Sandford's study shows how pupils often fail to realise the limited amount of information that can be shown on an atlas map, with the result that they make unwarranted inferences about a country.

Sandford's general conclusion was that map realism was not highly developed in most pupils, and that it varied with the age of the pupils and the course being followed. Pupils in the third and fourth forms achieved higher scores than those in the first and second forms in each subtest as well as in the test as a whole, especially in items relating to the understanding of symbols, the selection of information from the map, and concepts of number, length and height. Pupils following O-level courses scored more highly than those taking CSE courses, who in turn obtained better scores than non-examination pupils. Sandford also found that boys performed better than girls on most items and on the test as a whole. Sandford concluded that pupils' facility in the use of atlases was largely confined to locating named features and using basic techniques involving co-ordinates, direction and scale. He concluded that mechanical proficiency in these tasks was

insufficient if pupils were to have a real understanding of
the concepts underlying atlas maps. He was convinced that
pupils needed to master large scale maps before they handled
atlas maps, which would otherwise lack meaning for them.

Maps and Photographs

The communication system, consisting of a transmitter, channel
and receiver, can be applied to another medium of communication, the aerial photograph, which bears many similarities to
the map. Essential properties of a map are those of location
(for communicating positions), scale (for communicating
distances), projection (for communicating directions) and a
set of symbols (for communicating information about landscape
features). These four properties are also present in vertical
aerial photographs although they are not explicit and have to
be inferred. A vertical aerial photograph is in effect a
special kind of map. Its projection is parallel to the plane
of the landscape, its symbolism is entirely pictorial, it
shows the location of features and it has a scale, even if
this is not explicitly stated.

Some interesting experiments using vertical aerial photographs with six-year-old children from different cultures were
carried out by Blaut and Stea (1971). They believe that children of school-entering age are able to deal with map-like
information provided they do not have to read words or symbols.
Although a vertical aerial photograph does not possess a
statement of scale, projection or legend, these may be inferred
through comparison of the photograph with the area it represents and the objects on it. Accordingly Blaut and Stea
used such photographs to test the ability of pre-literate
children to read maps. The children tested in their first
experiment were 107 six-year-old children from the reception
classes of schools in Worcester, Massachusetts. Nearly all
of the children were apparently able to identify features on
an aerial photograph. Nineteen of the 107 Worcester children
were then asked to trace the outline of some houses and roads
from the photograph. When they had done so the photograph
was withdrawn and the children's attention was distracted for
a minute. They were then asked to name the shapes they had
drawn and colour the houses red and the roads yellow. Each
child was subsequently asked to draw in pencil the route he
would follow by road from one house to another. Sixteen of
the nineteen children were able to perform all tasks satis-
factorily and this led Blaut and Stea to claim that six-year-
olds can read iconic or pictorial maps.

Similar experiments were conducted with 20 six-year-old
children in the town of Rio Piedras in Puerto Rico and 58 of
the same age in an isolated peasant community in a mountainous

district on the island of St. Vincent in the West Indies,
where children had no contact with maps, television, films and
other pictorial representations of landscapes. Again the
results tend to suggest that map reading ability, as evidenced
by tasks carried out on vertical aerial photographs, appears
to be independent of the cultural setting in which children
live. Blaut and Stea claim that a 'natural' form of map
learning occurs as part of the normal development process in
young children. It is necessary to remember, however, that the
kind of map reading which the children were asked to attempt
was fairly simple. They were merely asked whether they could
recognise certain shapes on an aerial photograph as being
houses and roads, whether they could remember what their
tracings of these objects represented, and whether they could
indicate how to get from one house to another by road. They
were also handling representation of concrete objects with
which they would have been familiar. Nevertheless it does
seem from these experiments that young children can perceive
what the more prominent (discrete) shapes and lines represent
on a vertical aerial photograph, provided that they realise
what the photograph is meant to show. The claim by Blaut and
Stea that this ability appears to develop naturally in different cultures also needs to be treated with caution. When
the 58 St. Vincent children were asked to identify features
on the aerial photograph, the mean score per child was only
1.4 features, whereas with the 107 Worcester children the
mean score was 6.4 features. This would suggest that there
are considerable variations in the ability of children from
different cultures to perform this task.

In an experiment undertaken in a Cambridgeshire village
by Dale (1971) 40 children aged 6 to 11 years were shown a
vertical aerial photograph and a map of their own village,
both on a scale of 1:5,000 (approximately 12 inches to one
mile). Only 14 children (35%) realised that the area shown
was that of their own village. When 20 children were told
that the photograph showed their own village and asked to
identify 15 features on it, their combined score was 210 (70%)
out of a maximum of 300. The failure score of 90 (30%) was
rather heavily weighted by the relatively low scores of children below the age of 9 years. Children over the age of 9
seemed able to describe most of the prominent features shown
on the photograph, although it must be remembered that the
photograph was of an area with which they were familiar. They
might not have scored so well if the photograph had shown an
area that was not known to them. The children in this
experiment were also provided with a map on the same scale as
the aerial photograph and asked to say which they preferred.
Most children preferred the photograph to the map, although
there was little difference between the scores of children who
used the photograph and those who used the map. Dale con-

cluded that the main difficulty encountered by children in reading a map or aerial photograph was in forming a mental picture of the area which they could relate to the corresponding document in front of them.

Oblique as distinct from vertical aerial photographs present problems of a much higher order of magnitude, especially when pupils attempt to correlate features on them with the corresponding features on a map of the same area. The main problem is that of taking into account the variable scale of the oblique aerial photograph compared with the fixed scale of the map. A vertical aerial photograph approximates to a map, whilst an oblique aerial photograph represents a view from a high point such as the top of a hill in a rural area or the top of a tall block of flats in an urban area. The mental operations which are needed to correlate information on a map with that on an oblique aerial photograph present considerable difficulties even for pupils who have reached the stage of formal operational thinking.

Problems encountered by pupils in correlating an oblique aerial photograph with an Ordnance Survey map have been investigated by Boardman and Towner (1980). In their study of 578 pupils aged 15 to 16 years in their final year of statutory education in twelve Birmingham schools they presented the pupils with an oblique aerial photograph of the town of Tamworth, a sketch of the photograph and a 1:50,000 scale map of the town and its surrounding area. The map was chosen because it contained a small town surrounded by an area of gentle relief and was fairly typical of lowland Britain. The built-up environment which occupied most of the photograph was considered to be more familiar than a predominantly rural environment to the pupils in the urban schools tested. The edge of the town could be seen on the air photograph and certain dominant features in the town could be identified on the map. The pupils were asked to state the direction in which the camera was pointing when the photograph was taken. Subsequent questions asked the pupils to use the map to give the names of six features indicated on the sketch and identifiable on the map, six figure grid references for two locations, and the number of an A-class road. They were also asked to estimate the distance between points on the upper and lower edges of the photograph. The results are shown in Table 2.2.

It will be seen that the identification of the direction in which the camera was pointing proved to be quite difficult for most pupils. Whilst two-thirds of the O-level pupils could identify the direction (east) correctly, only one-third of CSE and GYSL pupils could do so. Many pupils appeared to assume automatically that the camera was pointing north and they remained north-orientated while attempting to correlate features on the photograph with the corresponding ones on the map. This accounted for the difficulty which many pupils experienced in identifying the six features. It was possible to identify the first feature, a castle, from the photograph alone and most pupils did so successfully. The remaining five features, however, all required the pupils to correlate the photograph with the map and read names, such as recreation ground, from it. Fewer pupils could manage this task and only the more able could correlate photograph with map in order to give grid references for two specific locations, or the number of the road. It also proved difficult for pupils to estimate the distance between the points on the upper and lower edges of the photograph because considerable skill was needed in lining up the edges of the photograph with corresponding lines on the map before the distance could be calculated.

Follow-up interviews were subsequently conducted individually with 91 of the 578 pupils who took the test (a 15 per cent sample). In these interviews the pupils were not initially asked to orientate the map and photograph but instead were asked to point to several prominent features on both. They were then asked to turn either the map or photograph until they both pointed in the same direction. All pupils managed to orientate map and photograph correctly after being given some help, but not all gave the correct answer (east) for the direction in which the camera was pointing. Although they had rotated the map or photograph through 90 degrees, some pupils remained north-orientated and gave the answer north or north-east. Some others confused east and west and gave the answer west. Pupils also generally overestimated the area of that part of the map which was shown on the photograph. Thus it was common for pupils to think that the whole town was shown on the photograph whereas only part of the town actually appeared on it.

Reference has been made to various studies in this chapter in order to draw attention to some of the difficulties which pupils encounter in reading and interpreting maps and photographs. Yet these two documents are widely used in geography lessons and the ability to handle them is of crucial importance if children are to acquire competence in graphicacy. Methods of teaching the essential ideas and basic skills of graphicacy form the subject of the next two chapters.

TABLE 2.2 SCORES ON MAP AND AERIAL PHOTOGRAPH CORRELATION

	O-LEVEL			CSE			GYSL			TOTAL		
	BOYS n=118 %	GIRLS n=91 %	TOTAL n=209 %	BOYS n=120 %	GIRLS n=83 %	TOTAL n=203 %	BOYS n=106 %	GIRLS n=60 %	TOTAL n=166 %	BOYS n=344 %	GIRLS n=234 %	TOTAL n=578 %
DIRECTION	71	58	66	41	23	33	30	32	31	48	39	44
FEATURE 1	94	91	93	77	61	71	79	62	73	84	73	79
FEATURE 2	61	43	53	24	13	20	17	12	15	35	24	30
FEATURE 3	47	36	43	23	14	20	14	3	10	29	20	25
FEATURE 4	69	56	64	39	18	30	32	12	25	47	31	41
FEATURE 5	60	53	57	33	17	27	24	10	19	39	29	35
FEATURE 6	45	23	35	16	10	13	17	7	13	26	14	21
GRID REF 1	71	48	61	29	13	23	23	7	17	42	25	35
GRID REF 2	75	47	63	32	22	27	19	5	14	42	27	36
ROAD	85	59	74	43	26	36	36	22	31	55	38	48
DISTANCE	58	34	47	21	11	17	21	8	16	33	19	28

Source: Boardman and Towner (1979)

3 The View from Above

Methods of teaching four basic concepts which children have to
grasp if they are to understand maps — direction, location,
scale and symbolism — are discussed in this chapter. They are
presented in roughly increasing order of difficulty and should
be within the ability of most children by the time they reach
the upper forms of the primary school. In view of the wide
differences in ability among children, however, and the
variations in attainment indicated by the studies discussed in
the previous chapter, it is only possible to specify the
approximate ages at which children should be capable of understanding certain ideas about maps or mastering specific skills
in using them. Nevertheless the sequence of teaching and
learning advocated is influenced to a large extent by the
qualitatively different stages of thought identified by Piaget
and in particular children's concepts of space from topological
through projective to Euclidean, as discussed in Chapter 1.
It also takes into account the findings of the studies reported
in Chapter 2. Children clearly have to be able to read the
words on maps, and direction, location and scale are all
essentially applications of mathematical concepts to another
area of the curriculum. Children's progress in graphicacy is
heavily dependent upon their competence in literacy and
numeracy.

Direction

Children soon learn to find their way about school by walking
from the entrance to their own classrooms and to other parts of
the school such as the hall. They should be encouraged to
give directions to each other and to visitors. Progress is
clearly dependent upon children's increasing mastery of
language, particularly in giving and receiving oral instructions.
These can be recorded on tape and children can carry cassette
tape recorders on their journeys around the school or playground, following such instructions as 'leave the room, turn
left, walk to the end of the corridor, turn right'. In the

playground children can follow routes marked out as large
arrows on the ground. It is particularly important that
children learn to distinguish left from right readily, as some
children of secondary school age still confuse the two and in
a few this persists into adult life.

Subsequently children can make simple drawings to show
routes on paper. These can start in the classroom, the
drawings showing the route from the door to a child's desk.
The children can then make further drawings to show the route
from the school entrance to the hall or classroom. There is
no need for these to be accurate. As noted earlier, younger
children will draw simple topological maps showing points
joined by lines. They are making use of the elementary
relationship of proximity and its related one of separation.

Before children learn the points of the compass they
should be familiar with the process of rotation through
turning. The ideas of quarter-turn, half-turn, three-quarter-
turn and complete turn will have been encountered in learning
to tell the time, using conventional as distinct from digital
clocks and watches, and these are fundamental to the understanding of direction. The points of the compass should be
taught initially as the four cardinal points, north, east,
south and west, until children have thoroughly mastered them.
It is quite common for children to confuse east and west,
particularly if they are unsure about the distinction between
left and right, and this confusion may persist if it is not
mastered properly at an early age. The common description
of lines or routes as 'east-west' (right-left) rather than as
'west-east' (left-right) probably encourages the persistence
of errors with these two cardinal points. Mnemonics such as
'Never Eat Shredded Wheat' or 'Naughty Elephants Squirt
Water' may help children to remember the cardinal points
correctly. The word 'we' will help to avoid confusion
between west and east, as will a mental image of the map of
Britain showing Wales on the west and England on the east.

Children should be taken out into the playground and
taught to orientate themselves so that they know the
directions in which north, east, south and west lie. Whilst
doing this they can rotate on the spot through a complete
circle, preferably using a compass. They can then walk
round the playground with a compass and note the direction in
which they are facing at certain points. They can go round
the outside of the school building, and decide which of the
exterior walls are north-facing and which are south-facing.
This exercise can be linked to the relative warmth of south-
facing walls and rooms when the sun is out, and the corresponding coolness of the north-facing side of the building.

THE VIEW FROM ABOVE

The other walls can be linked to the observation of relative warmth at certain times of the day, as the sun apparently rises in the east, giving early morning warmth to east-facing walls, and sets in the west, giving late afternoon warmth to west-facing walls.

The learning of the four intermediate points of the compass ought not to cause much difficulty for children if they remember that the north and south points always precede the east and west points. Thus the order is north-east, south-east, (not east-south), south-west, and north-west (not west-north). Similar exercises to those advocated for the cardinal points can be undertaken by children once the intermediate points are known. These can usefully be reinforced by frequent reference to the weather forecast and map on television. Children should take their own readings of wind direction if a weather vane is available. In particular they should learn that wind direction is always stated as the direction from which, and not to which, the wind is blowing.

Once children have grasped these eight points they can learn the full sixteen points of the compass. They only have to remember the rule that the four cardinal points are stated first and to these are added the adjacent intermediate points. Thus the remaining eight points are north-north-east, east-north-east, east-south-east, south-south-east, south-south-west, west-south-west, west-north-west, and north-north-west. In practice use of these in everyday life is mainly confined to weather forecasts.

The children's work in mathematics will determine whether they can convert compass points into degrees and learn to read bearings. In particular they will need to understand that angles are measures of the amount of turn and they should be able to use a circular as well as semi-circular protractor. If they are familiar with right angles and the division of the circle into 360 degrees, they will soon learn that the bearings of the cardinal points are 090, 180, and 270 degrees and that 0 and 360 degrees are the same bearing. Similarly, they should grasp that each of the intermediate points is half a right angle, giving bearings of 045, 135, 225 and 315 degrees. Further subdivision into quarter right angles and the reading of bearings at $22\frac{1}{2}$ degree intervals will depend upon the children's facility with number and the extent to which they have used protractors in mathematical work.

It is important that children reinforce their knowledge of compass points through practice. In the classroom they should learn to point correctly to the various directions. They should be able to state the direction in which they are moving when they walk from one part of the classroom to another. They can do the same by going into the playground and walking round the school building or following routes marked out on the ground with chalk.

The children should then use their skills in conjunction with a map of the roads around the school. It is recommended that this could be done with the aid of the road pattern shown on an A to Z map and duplicated by the teacher with a route marked on it. The children can be taken on a short walk and record the direction in which they are travelling as they walk along each road and turn at each road junction. They can subsequently be shown the A to Z map from which the road pattern is taken (Figure 3.1). This is a useful map to which to introduce children at an early age because it shows only roads and their names, without the distracting details of buildings and other features. It is also the kind of map that they are most likely to encounter in everyday life.

Although the points of the compass as drawn on a sheet of paper constitute an apparently straightforward idea, it should not be assumed that children will automatically understand their true meaning. It is not easy at first for children to appreciate that north is always the same direction irrespective of their own position. They can work out, for example, that the direction of their school from home is west. If they walk past the school, however, continuing in the same direction, then the school lies to the east of them. It is important to teach and reinforce through practice that the direction from one place to another is always the direction from which they are standing towards which they are looking.

In order to develop their sense of direction primary school children can be encouraged to draw from memory a free-hand map of a local walk, such as that from home to school. Such a map, known as a cognitive map, is a representation of the child's image of an area which is too large for him to see all at once. The cognitive maps of young children are likely to be topological in structure, consisting simply of lines representing roads joining up points representing places. Although such maps are unlikely to be very accurate, they do have useful diagnostic and informative functions (Catling, 1978b). Used as a diagnostic instrument they provide the teacher with insights into the child's perceptions, representations and learning. They can help the teacher to discern the level of the child's spatial conception and graphic representation of a familiar environment, the procedure being similar to that used by Piaget, Inhelder and Szeminska (1960). A cognitive map also provides the teacher with an informative guide to the focal points of the local environment which are important to children, or with which they are particularly familiar.

The drawing of cognitive maps, however, can also be used as a teaching technique. When children have drawn from memory a map of their route to school, they can think about the way they came and discuss it or write about it, thus clarifying in their own minds the route they used. On the following day they can look more carefully at their route ,whilst walking to school, noting especially orientation and direction. Upon returning to their original maps, they can decide whether they are accurate, and if necessary correct or redraw them. If several children take similar routes to school they can compare one another's maps for accuracy and orient- ation. If children take many different routes to school they can see whether they are able to understand one another's maps and the routes shown on them. In any case children should subsequently compare their freehand maps with the A to Z road map of the local area and assess the accuracy and orientation of their own maps alongside it. Accurate orientation necess- arily involves a knowledge of the points of the compass as an aid to direction. Marking the north point on maps helps to develop the children's conception not only of north but also of the other points. Cognitive maps should always be compared with the real maps that the children are likely to use later.

In the classroom the concept of direction can be developed with the aid of a globe. Direction can be confined to the four cardinal points with younger children, who observe that countries are north or south of the equator, and east or west of Britain. If a globe is not available a simple atlas map may be used provided that the compass points are clearly indicated on it. Children are easily confused when the com- pass points are not shown, even though the convention is to place north at the top of the map (Bartz, 1965). Children should be able to determine the direction in which a certain town lies from their own, or the direction in which they would have to travel to go on holiday to a coastal resort. Simple topological maps, in which points are connected by straight lines, are ideal for map exercises involving direction.

Location

The concept of the map as a plan can be introduced to children at an early age. Children in the lower stages of primary education can make their own models of different buildings, such as a church, a hall, a few shops and several houses. Cardboard can be used to make the buildings, or they can be constructed from matchboxes or other small containers. If each child makes one building it will not take a class long to produce a collection large enough to represent an imaginary

THE VIEW FROM ABOVE

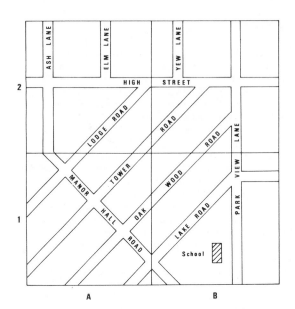

FIGURE 3.1. DIRECTION USING A ROAD MAP

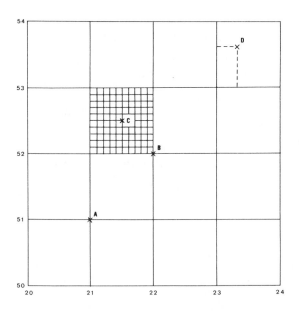

FIGURE 3.2. LOCATION USING GRID REFERENCES

44

village or suburban shopping centre. The children then
arrange their buildings on a base of strong cardboard or thin
hardboard and add roads.

When all the children in the class have placed their
buildings in position, they are told that their model has to
be stored away with the base propped up against a wall. They
are asked how all the buildings can be placed in exactly the
same position on the following day. The children can then
see that they should draw round the base of each building before it is removed and label its position with a number. When
all the buildings have been taken away what is left is a map
of the imaginary village or shopping centre. The children
then see the map placed upright against the wall and realise
that it is a permanent record which is retained no matter
which way up it is turned. The village or shopping centre is
reassembled the next day so as to give the children practice
in placing buildings in position at specified locations.
Children are then to be asked questions about it, for example,
what would they see when walking from one end of the village
to the other, or what shops would they pass when walking along
the street? The buildings are removed again and the same
questions are asked, so that the children realise that information about a place can be obtained from the map alone.

By this stage children will have learnt to appreciate
the relative location of objects and the relationships between
them. They will realise where one building on the map lies in
relation to the others. In other words, they are developing
an understanding of projective space. The question of stating
precise location now arises. Each side of the map can be
divided into units of equal length and lines drawn across the
map to create squares. The squares along one side are lettered
A, B, C, D, E, etc. and those along the adjacent side are
numbered 1, 2, 3, 4, 5, etc. The positions of objects in
different squares can then be given by using a letter followed
by a number, such as A1, B3, C4, D2, E5, etc.

Children can practise using letters and numbers with the
A to Z road map which adopts this system for identifying
squares (Figure 3.1). They should be taught to refer to the
index of road names, which gives the letter and number of the
square in which each road is located. Thus the children have
to search for the required road within that square. Pairs of
children can play taxi games in which one child is a taxi
driver finding his way from a given place to a destination
specified by the other child, roads being named on the
journey. Alternatively pairs of children can play police
games with a controller directing a panda car to a specific
road on the map.

After searching squares for the names of roads children
will soon see the advantages of using a more precise method of
locating places. So far they have used squares to locate
places; children should subsequently learn to use grid lines
as reference systems. The ability to use two criteria each
arranged in series to locate a place or object is one which
develops in children towards the end of the stage of concrete
operational thinking.

It is recommended that every school should possess an
Ordnance Survey map of the area in which the school is
situated on a scale of 1:1,250 (50 inches to one mile) or
1:2,500 (25 inches to one mile). Since these are large
documents it will be advisable to cut them up into smaller
pieces, each measuring 10 cm by 10 cm, so that they can be
pasted onto workcards. This is not just to make them easier
to handle. Children tend to be interested in detail on maps
and such interest can be channelled to good effect by isolating
small areas for children to study (Catling, 1979). Two copies
of each map are therefore required: one for wall display and
another for cutting up. Schools can purchase maps direct
from the Ordnance Survey at discount rates if the maps are
supplied for teaching purposes and are to remain the property
of the school. In view of the high cost of large scale maps
it is worth noting that the Ordnance Survey's copyright licence
fees for local authorities include an extra cost element to
cover educational map copying. Consequently schools supported
or maintained by a local authority may make copies within
prescribed size limits from the maps they purchase.

When a piece of map has been pasted onto a workcard the
grid lines should be numbered along the top, bottom and sides,
always giving two digits for each line. When children start
to use their workcards their attention should be drawn to these
numbers. In particular they should note that the numbering
starts in the lower left hand corner and moves to the right
and upwards in exactly the same way as the axes of graphs
drawn in mathematics. The difference with maps is simply that
the lines are named eastings and northings. Once children
have learnt the cardinal points of the compass they should
readily distinguish eastings and northings. These are commonly confused by children of all ages and so the reasons for
the names need to be carefully explained. The starting point
is always the south-west corner of the map. The vertical lines
are drawn east of this point and so are called eastings. Their
numbers are printed at the ends of the lines along the lower
and upper margins of the map. Similarly the horizontal lines
are drawn north of the same point and so are called northings.
Their numbers are printed at the ends of the lines along both
sides of the map. The intersection of an easting and northing

is the grid reference not only of that point but of the
square that lies to the east and north of it. Emphasis should
be placed on the importance of giving eastings before northings
as they are frequently given the wrong way round by children.
A simple but useful memory aid is that E comes before N in the
alphabet. Another is to tell children to remember to 'walk
along the corridor before they climb the stairs', so that they
read off the number along the lower margin of the map before
the number along the side margin of the map. Thus in Figure
3.2 the grid references of points A and B are 2151 and 2252,
whilst points C and D are located in squares 2152 and 2353.

Children can then learn to locate points precisely within
squares by means of six figure grid references. For this
purpose each side of the square is divided into tenths, giving
a total of 100 smaller squares within the larger one. The
lines bounding the squares are numbered from 1 to 9 eastwards
and from 1 to 9 northwards. These numbers are added to the
two figure eastings and northings. Thus in Figure 3.2 the six
figure reference for point C is 215 525 and that for point D
is 233 536. In the early stages of practice in giving grid
references the children will find it helpful to draw the 100
small squares on tracing paper and superimpose this tracing
on each large grid square, as is done for point C. It can be
explained to the children that these small squares are not
printed on maps because they would conceal detail on them,
and in practice the divisions into tenths are estimated, as is
done for point D. It should also be pointed out to children
that if an object lies on an easting the third figure of a six
figure grid reference is 0, and if an object lies at the intersection of an easting and northing, both the third and sixth
figures will be 0. Hence in figure 3.2 the six figure
reference for point A is 210 510 and for point B is 220 520.

The use of co-ordinates can be extended to latitude and
longitude with older primary school children if they have
learnt to make angular measurements in mathematics. By
examining a globe children will see that the circumference
can be divided into 360 degrees like any other circle. Lines
of longitude are numbered east and west of longitude zero
(Greenwich) through a semi-circle, however, so that 180
degrees E and 180 degrees W are the same line. In the case
of latitude lines are numbered from latitude zero (the Equator)
northwards and southwards through a quarter-circle, so that
90 degrees N and 90 degrees S are the north and south poles
respectively. Angular measurements from the centre of a
sphere should not be attempted with children until they have
had considerable experience with circles and angles in mathematics. In order to use the index of an atlas, however,
children will need to know that each degree is divided into

60 minutes. It can be difficult to estimate minutes between two lines of latitude and longitude, and it is therefore advisable that children should first have adequate practice in using six figure grid references on large scale maps. Children should also remember that latitude is always given before longitude. This can be a source of confusion because in grid references eastings are given before northings. If children are to locate places successfully it is essential that the atlas maps they use are simple and clear, with names printed prominently and widely spaced.

Scale

Children learn that objects are made to scale when they play with toys. Model cars are scaled down versions of real cars, and doll's houses are miniature replicas of real ones. It is interesting to note the way in which children as they grow older do not mix models built on different scales, rejecting them as being 'too big' or 'too small', and thus indicating the emergent appreciation of scale. The popularity of Lego as the successor to Meccano shows the continuing enthusiasm with which boys use model building materials. It is not known, however, whether this sex differentiation in childhood — boys making models and girls playing with dolls — is in any way related to the apparently greater development of spatial ability in boys.

Building upon their experience of playing with toys, primary school children learn through mathematics to record measurement with increasing accuracy. These measuring tasks help children to develop greater confidence in the use of rulers and tapes. They should become familiar with both imperial and metric units as both are used on maps in everyday life. Direct comparisons between say, centimetres and inches, or metres and yards, will help children to appreciate the relationship between metric and imperial units of measurement.

Several small objects can be used to show that some items can be drawn in plan form without reduction. Thus one penny, two pence, ten pence, twenty pence and fifty pence coins can be placed on a piece of paper and lines drawn around them. Then the children can be asked how they could show on a piece of paper the shape and size of a book which is larger than the paper itself. They will see that reduction to half size will be sufficient, so the children have only to grasp that each 2 cm along the edge of the book is represented by 1 cm on their scale drawing. The need for the children to measure both the length and the width of the book will help them to understand the principle that all plans are drawn in two dimensions. The same book can then be drawn to quarter scale, 4 cm along the edge of the book being represented by 1 cm on the plan. This will introduce children to the idea of decreasing scale and the need to select an appropriate scale for the task in hand.

The next stage in scale drawing is for children to draw plans of the tops of their desks or tables. Taking into account the size of their paper, they will need to decide on a suitable scale after careful thought and discussion. Thus if each top measures 60 cm by 45 cm an appropriate scale might be quarter size, 1 cm on the plan representing 4 cm on the desk top. It is important to emphasise the use and meaning of the word 'represents' to the children. To say that '1 cm equals 4 cm' is mathematically incorrect. In practice the word 'to' can be used for the sake of brevity, the scale being described as '1 cm to 4 cm'. Having drawn a desk top, the children can then add to their plan one or two objects placed on it, such as a pencil, ruler and book, all drawn to scale. There is no need for the objects to be placed in the precise positions on the plan since they are themselves moveable.

With this scale drawing task completed, the children can attempt a plan of the classroom. This should be within the capabilities of primary school children aged 10—11 years provided that they use a carefully chosen scale and are led through the task in steps. If the classroom is 9 metres long and 6 metres wide an appropriate scale might be 2 cm to represent 1 metre. When each measurement has been taken with a 10 metre tape, therefore, the resulting figure has simply to be doubled and converted to centimetres when drawn on metric graph paper. Pairs of children can take turns in using the tape and the teacher can build up a sketch plan on the blackboard. It is important that the blackboard sketch is drawn with the back of the room at the bottom of the blackboard and the front of the room at the top, so that as the children look at the sketch it is the same way up as their own plans. Once the rectangle has been drawn and the doors inserted, various pieces of furniture can be added. Depending on the ability of individuals in the class, such features as the blackboard and cupboards can be measured and drawn in their correct positions (Figure 3.3). If the insertion of all desks would take too long, then the children can insert only their own desks by measuring distances from adjacent walls. They should realise, however, that if only selected desks are inserted their plans are only partially complete.

The rooms and furniture in many schools will have been made to imperial rather than metric measurements. This raises the fundamental question of which measurements should be used in drawing the plan. If the children have been accustomed to working with metric units in their mathematics lessons, it is clearly desirable that they should continue to do so in scale drawing. If they have used both metric and imperial units

49

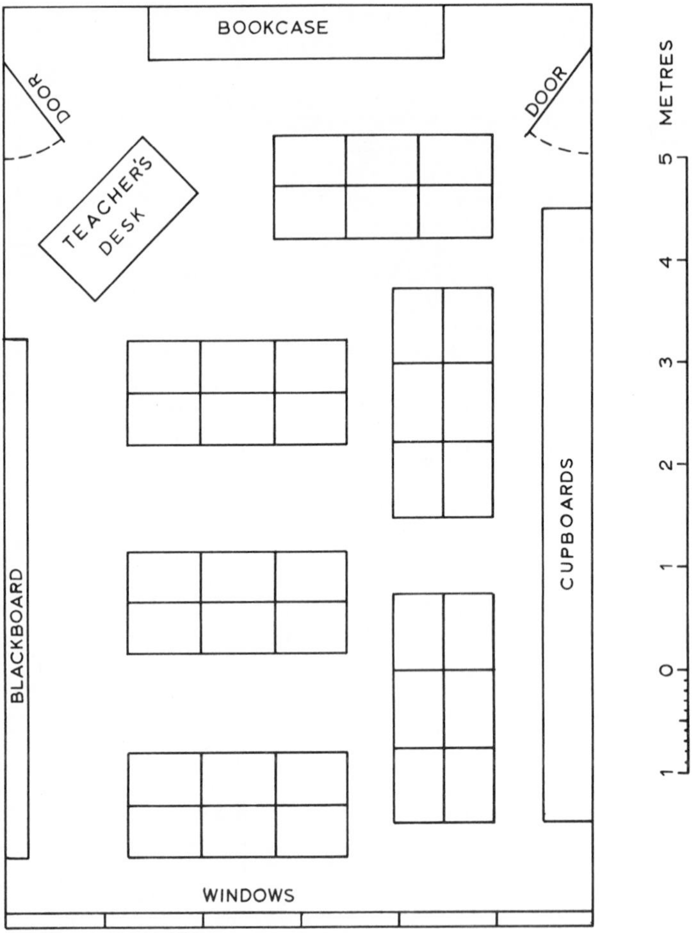

THE VIEW FROM ABOVE

FIGURE 3.3. PLAN OF A CLASSROOM

there could be advantages in using imperial measurements for drawing the classroom and furniture. In this case it is important that the squared paper they draw on is in imperial units, such as quarter-inch squares. Attempting to measure in feet and inches, and converting to graph paper divided into centimetres and millimetres, will only lead to confusion.

A linear scale should be added to this first attempt at map drawing. Although a graduated line from zero to the five or six metre mark will serve its purpose, it can be useful to extend it to the left of the zero mark and divide the resulting unit into tenths. This enables metres and fractions of metres to be read off without dividing up the entire scale.

If further work on scale plan drawing is required, a map of the exterior of the school can be attempted. This will reinforce the idea of maps drawn on ever-decreasing scales as the size of the area to be mapped becomes larger. A scale of 1 centimetre to 1 metre may be used for small buildings, but for larger ones it may be necessary to reduce it so that 1 centimetre represents 2 metres or perhaps 5 metres.

The emphasis can then change from drawing plans to using them. The children can be presented with a plan of the interior of the school drawn to scale, similar to that in Figure 3.4. This can be the basis of exercises in which children make measurements from the plan and convert these to the real-life measurements. Thus they can find out from the plan the actual length and width of the school hall as well as the approximate measurements of individual classrooms. The same plan can be used for revising direction through the identification of north, south, east and west facing walls or rooms.

Children can be taught to express scales in terms of ratios if these have been covered in mathematics. Thus in the first exercise attempted by the children the plan of the book was drawn at a scale of 1:2, and in the next exercise the plan of the desk top was drawn at a scale of 1:4. The plan of the classroom might have been drawn at a scale of 1:50 and that of the school at a scale of 1:250. The term ratio is preferred to representative fraction because of its simplicity for younger children.

Having worked with a series of plan drawings at progressively smaller scales, the children can return to the workcards containing the pieces of Ordnance Survey maps on the 1:1,250 or 1:2,500 scales. They can undertake numerous measuring exercises on these maps, working out, for example, the approximate lengths of gardens or rows of houses, and distances along roads between home and school. In this way they will soon

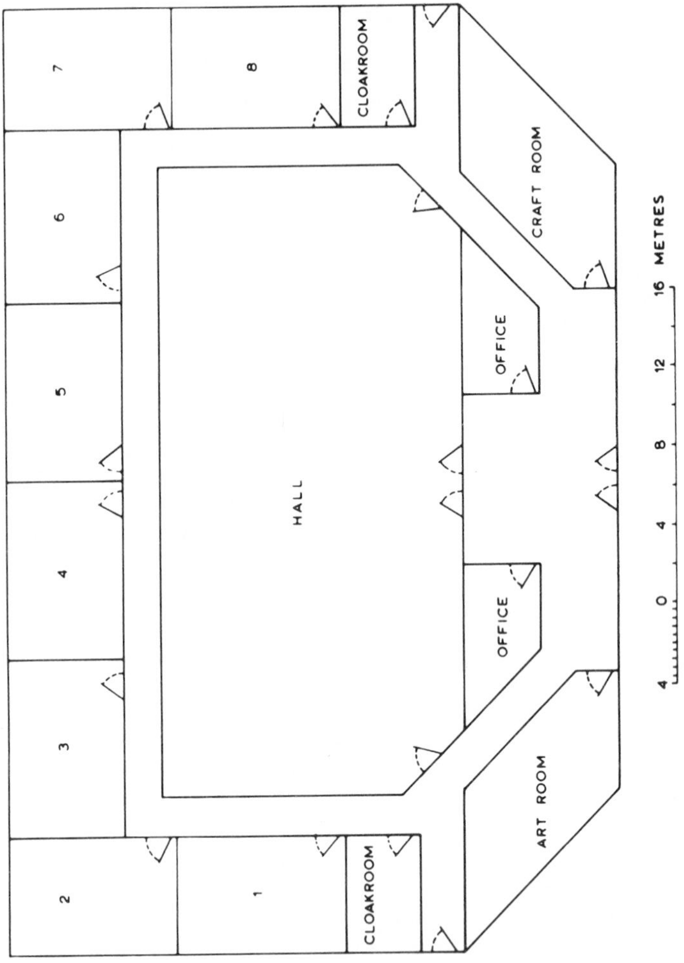

FIGURE 3.4. PLAN OF A SCHOOL

begin to appreciate the meaning of measurements such as '50 metres' or distances such as 'half a mile'.

Further workcards on scale can be prepared using other maps produced by the Ordnance Survey, as described in the next section. The size of the maps on all scales makes it desirable for the teacher to cut them up into smaller square or rectangular pieces and paste them on to workcards before children compare them. When preparing workcards it will be useful to start with 10 cm by 10 cm squares of the same area cut from the 1:1,250, 1:2,500 and 10,000 maps. If children place these alongside each other they will, by measurement, be able to see that the 1:1,250 extract represents an area 125 metres by 125 metres, the 1:2,500 extract an area 250 metres by 250 metres, and the 1:10,000 extract an area 1 km by 1 km. This kilometre grid square can then be compared with the corresponding grid squares on the 1:25,000 and 1:50,000 maps, which measure 4 cm by 4 cm and 2 cm by 2 cm respectively. Finally they can compare a large grid square representing an area 10 km by 10 km on the 1:250,000 map with the corresponding 10 km grid squares on the 1:25,000 and 1:50,000 maps. Children should measure the distance between the same two points on maps of different scales and see that distance remains constant whilst scale changes. Examples of fieldwork involving the use of large scale maps in urban and rural areas are included in Chapter 7.

The use of maps on ever-decreasing scales can progress naturally from the 1:250,000 map to atlas maps. Children should again be able to compare the same area shown on maps drawn on different scales but this time on successive pages of their atlases. Thus a map drawn on a scale of 1 cm to 10 km (1:1,000,000) will show greater London on one page; a map on a scale of 1 cm to 40 km (1:4,000,000) will show the whole of south-east England; one on a scale of 1 cm to 80 km (1:8,000,000) will show the whole of England; and another on a scale of 1 cm to 200 km (1:20,000,000) will show much of western Europe. Since numbers of this magnitude are meaningless to children, they should use the scale lines on the maps to measure distances between places and also to measure the same distance on maps of different scales. As Bartz (1965) has noted, even when a map bears a linear scale children often do not refer to it. Most children take considerable time to develop a systematic procedure for using a linear scale. Scale expressed as a representative fraction is rarely understood immediately. If children compare maps on ever decreasing scales they will see that as the scale becomes smaller, so the number in the ratio becomes larger. Similarly, as the scale becomes smaller, so the area shown becomes larger.

The concept of scale as consistent proportional representation is one which many children experience difficulty
in mastering. It requires an understanding of Euclidean space,
which begins to develop in most children towards the end of
the stage of concrete operational thinking. As was noted in
Chapter 1, children begin to understand distance and proportion after the age of about 10 years, and both of the concepts are essential for an understanding of scale. In drawing
a scale plan children have to work out not only position and
distance, using a system of co-ordinates, but also perspective
and proportion, using a system of measurement conversion. The
concept of a diagrammatic layout incorporating all these properties, with accurate measurement of distance and proportional
reduction to scale as well as the correct positioning of
objects in relation to one another, is not completely mastered
by most children until they begin to make the transition to
formal operational thinking. Nevertheless essential ideas
about direction, location and scale should be understood by
most children by the time they complete their primary school
education (Catling, 1980). Work with less able children may
need to be taken at a much slower pace until the concepts are
fully understood. Approaches which geography teachers find
successful in extending basic skills in English and Mathematics with slow learning children in their first year of secondary education are available elsewhere (Boardman, 1982b).

Symbolism

When children have acquired the basic concepts of direction,
location and scale they will appreciate the need for the use
of symbols. It is important that they understand the reasons
for the use of symbols and this is best done by starting with
the large scale map of the local area and proceeding to maps
on ever-decreasing scales, the advantages of which have been
discussed elsewhere (Boardman, 1976a). Children who are
reaching the later phase of the stage of concrete operational
thought are developing an understanding of order of magnitude,
symmetrical relationships and constant reference systems.
This is an excellent time to introduce them to the symbolism
on a series of maps arranged according to size and scale.

The largest scale maps published by the Ordnance Survey,
those on the 1:1,250 scale (1 cm to 12.5 metres or 50 inches
to 1 mile), cover all urban areas of not less than 1,000
hectares containing a population of 20,000 or more. Each map
represents an area 500 metres by 500 metres and thus measures
40 cm by 40 cm. Buildings, roads and open spaces are shown
to scale, houses are numbered and roads are named. The next
largest scale maps, the 1:2,500 (1 cm to 25 metres or 25 inches
to 1 mile), cover smaller urban areas and all rural areas

except mountain and moorland. Each map normally covers an area of 2 km from west to east by 1 km from north to south and thus measures 80 cm by 40 cm. The detail shown is the same as that on the 1:1,250 scale series but reduced in size.

The 1:10,000 scale maps (1 cm to 100 metres or approximately 6 inches to 1 mile) are gradually replacing the former 1:10,560 series (6 inches to 1 mile) as part of the metrication programme. These are the largest scale maps to cover the whole of the country, including mountain and moorland areas, and to show contours. Most maps cover an area of 5 km by 5 km and thus measure 50 cm by 50 cm at the 1:10,000 scale. The shapes of buildings are generalised but roads are still named.

Pathfinder maps on the 1:25,000 scale (4 cm to 1 km or $2\frac{1}{2}$ inches to 1 mile) form one of the most popular and readily accessible series, being available in folded as well as flat form. Most Pathfinder maps cover an area 20 km ($12\frac{1}{2}$ miles) from west to east by 10 km ($6\frac{1}{4}$ miles) from north to south. They thus measure 80 cm by 40 cm and are twice the size of the 1:25,000 first series maps which they are replacing. Their appearance is made attractive by the use of colour: roads are shown in orange, areas of water in blue and woodland in green. As their name implies, Pathfinder maps are particularly useful for walkers because public rights of way are shown distinctively by means of broken green lines.

The most widely used maps are the Landranger series on the 1:50,000 scale (2 cm to 1 km or $1\frac{1}{4}$ inches to 1 mile) which have replaced the former 1:63,360 scale (1 inch to 1 mile) maps. Each Landranger map covers an area 40 km by 40 km (25 miles by 25 miles) and thus measures 80 cm by 80 cm. Features of the Landranger maps are redesigned symbols and a clearer type face than was used on the 1 inch to 1 mile maps. Built-up areas, for example, are lightly tinted instead of shaded grey and the square upper and lower case type face makes for greater legibility. Considerable use is made of colour to distinguish different kinds of roads, primary roads being shown in red, secondary roads in brown, minor roads in yellow, and motorways in blue. Rights of way such as footpaths and bridleways are shown, and tourist information such as camping and caravan sites, picnic areas and viewpoints is included.

Routemaster maps on the 1:250,000 scale (1 cm to 2.5 km or 1 inch to 4 miles) form a useful link between the large scale topographical maps outlined above and small scale atlas maps. The whole country is covered by only nine maps, which thus provide a good series for the motorist. For this purpose most roads are shown, motorways, primary and secondary routes being distinctively coloured blue, red and brown respectively.

The shapes of towns are shown in generalised form and lightly tinted in yellow.

By close examination of the detail on specific squares of the maps on these different scales children will then begin to realise the need for symbols. These can be classified into three categories: points, such as posts and pylons; lines, such as roads and rivers; and areas, such as fields and factories. The need for point symbols is best illustrated by reference to a particular building. On a 1:1,250 or 1:2,500 map the exact shape of a church is shown because the building is drawn precisely to scale. The same church should then be located on the 1:10,000 map. It will be seen that the reduction in scale to one quarter that of the 1:2,500 map makes it impossible to show the exact shape of the building. Instead it appears only as a generalised shape, a black or grey rectangle. The church should next be located on the 1:25,000 map and it will be seen that the further reduction in scale means that the building is now shown as a symbol: a square with a cross if the church has a tower and a circle with a cross if it has a spire, or a cross on its own if it has neither. The symbol attempts to portray the two basic plan features of the church: the tower or spire, and the nave and chancel. The size of the symbol on the map, however, occupies much more space on the paper than it would do if the building had been drawn to scale. There is a still greater exaggeration with the corresponding symbol on a 1:50,000 map. Indeed, the size of the symbol is out of all proportion to the area of the ground it covers in reality. A prominent symbol on the map thus represents a building which is not necessarily very conspicuous among many other buildings on the ground. Unless children realise this they may experience difficulty in matching up a map with the corresponding features out of doors or in correlating a map with an aerial photograph. On the 1:250,000 map the church is too small to show as a separate building.

A similar procedure of working with maps of the same area on every-decreasing scales can be used with line symbols. On 1:1,250 and 1:2,500 maps roads are not only named but are shown to scale at their correct width. On 1:10,000 maps this is no longer possible and a standard width is employed, large enought to permit the names of the roads to appear, although dual carriageways are still shown. Road names do not appear on 1:25,000 maps and an orange colouring is introduced for major roads. The width of roads is greatly exaggerated on 1:50,000 maps. A two-lane A-class road shown in red occupies a width of $\frac{1}{2}$ mm, which at this scale is equivalent to 25 m on the ground, the width of a six-lane motorway! And on a 1:250,000 map it is equivalent to the width of five motorways! It should also be pointed out to children that the colouring of

roads orange, red, brown, yellow and white on maps is purely
a convention. They often wonder why there is no resemblance
to the black or grey tarmac with which they are familiar. The
use of blue for motorways is particularly confusing because
this colour indicates water features elsewhere on the map.

Area symbols on maps of different scales can most easily
be compared by selecting an area of woodland. This is shown
on maps at all scales from 1:1,250 to 1:250,000, although some
generalisation of the boundary lines accompanies the reduction
in scale. Children should also look for differences in the
symbols used within the boundary lines. Thus copse is shown
on 1:10,000 maps and deciduous woodland is distinguished from
coniferous woodland on 1:25,000 maps, but on 1:50,000 and
1:250,000 maps all woodland is indicated only by plain green
layer colouring. The area covered by the same settlement on
maps of different scales can also be compared. Children can
indicate the extent of the settlement on the 1:1,250, 1:2,500
and 1:10,000 maps and then compare it with the generalised
boundary shown on the 1:25,000, 1:50,000 maps and 1:250,000
maps.

What has been said about symbols on Ordnance Survey maps
applies equally to atlas maps, except that there are fewer
variations between the symbols used on maps drawn on successively smaller scales. A dot represents a town on an atlas
map irrespective of the scale. Accordingly the area that the
dot covers on a small scale atlas map is out of all proportion
to the area that the town occupies on the ground. The same
is true of linear symbols like railways and rivers. Atlas
maps are also much more selective in the nature of the
information that they portray. Only the larger towns or main
railways and rivers are shown; smaller ones occupy the areas
between them shown as blank spaces on the map. The lettering
used for the names on a map is also very important. Bartz
(1965) emphasises that children are more conscious of the
names on the map than of any other element. Their understanding of much of the other symbolisation depends upon how
readily they see and understand the names. Familiarity with
a name, the alignment and spacing of letters and words, and
the type size, style and weight can all affect the ease with
which names are noticed and read. Noyes (1979) similarly
stresses that whilst the information content of a map is
important, the readiness with which this information is
obtained by the map user varies with legibility, which is
determined by the design of the map.

The various symbols used on maps of different scales
deserve careful consideration. Children need to be able to
perform two distinct tasks. They have to see or perceive the
symbol on the map, and then appreciate the concept for which

it stands. It is possible, for example, to perceive a red
line running across a map without necessarily realising that
it represents a main or A-class road. There is limited value
in asking children merely to copy a series of symbols, list
what they represent, and then learn them by heart. This may
be an opportunity to practise artistic skills but it requires
little thought. Furthermore, the features represented by some
symbols may never have been seen by the pupils. A church with
a tower or spire may perhaps be fairly easy to visualise, but
if the pupils have never seen a triangulation station or
visited a quarry, photographs should be used to present the
visual image. Symbols showing different kinds of vegetation,
such as heath, scrub and reeds, will usually need to be supplemented by specimens of these plants if they are to be truly
meaningful to children. There is also little to be gained
from asking pupils to find one or two examples of each symbol
on a map. This only encourages them to find objects in
isolation rather than in the setting in which they are located.

Since one of the main purposes for which maps are used in
adult life is as a means of finding the way from one place to
another, route finding exercises are valuable and purposeful.
Children should be given a starting point and a destination
which has to be reached. They should then follow the route
and describe what they would see on the way. This kind of
exercise can be made more difficult by specifying a particular
route to be followed and asking the pupils to describe what
they would see at particular grid references. They can also
measure the distance which would be covered and state the
direction in which they would be travelling between specific
points, thus reinforcing earlier work on scale, location and
direction.

4 The Third Dimension

An understanding of the representation of height, slope and
relief on a map is probably the aspect of graphicacy which is
most difficult to develop in the majority of children. Although young children will recognise hills and valleys shown
on pictures, the teaching of the representation of relief on
maps is usually best left until children are making the
transition from concrete to formal operational thinking. It
should be remembered that many of the children in the first
two years of secondary schools, or the corresponding years in
middle schools, will still be at the stage of concrete operational thought. Indeed some will not make the transition until much later. It is recommended that most of the work
discussed in this chapter, therefore, should normally be undertaken with children aged 11 to 13 in the lower part of the
secondary school or upper forms of the middle school. Throughout emphasis is placed on the use of teaching aids and the
involvement of children in practical activities to assist them
in understanding abstract ideas as they make the transition
from concrete to formal operational thinking. The methods
advocated are designed to help children to develop a true
understanding of height, slope and relief, and subsequently
to appreciate the three dimensional element in sketches and
photographs.

The Concept of Contours

When children have learnt to handle a large scale map of an
area familiar to them, such as that around the school, they
can mark on it at selected points the land which is higher than
the school building with a plus sign and land which is lower
with a minus sign. The higher land can then be distinguished
from the lower land by means of a line drawn on the map. This
boundary is in effect a contour line and the land above it can
be shaded, this being a simple form of layer shading. It is
important that the children do not think that the boundary line
represents some form of step or break in slope, and the fact

that they have plotted the line themselves should ensure that
they continue to recognise the slope as an even or smooth one.

In the classroom the concept of contours should always be
taught with the aid of models when children are still at the
stage of concrete operational thinking. Plasticine is very
useful for this purpose since it is relatively cheap and can
be moulded easily and quickly without, in the initial stages,
reference to specific heights. A large plasticine model of a
stretch of coastline should be moulded for class demonstration
purposes by the teacher. The lower quarter is in blue plasticine and the upper three quarters in green or some other
colour. It is placed in a standard transparent tank, the side
of which is marked with a scale graduated at regular intervals.
The base of the tank represents the dry shore at low tide.
Water is then poured into the tank to represent the incoming
tide until the first mark on the scale is reached. With an
old ball point pen or any pointed instrument the line of the
new sea level is marked on the plasticine model (Figure 4.1).
The sea level is then raised again until it reaches the second
mark on the scale. This should correspond with the junction
between the blue and green plasticine and represents high water
mark.

The class then has to imagine that sea level is rising
again under storm conditions and is beginning to flood the
coastal land. Water is poured into the tank until the next
mark on the scale is reached. A line is marked on the plasticine to represent the new sea level. Storm conditions continue
and more water is poured into the tank until the next mark is
reached. The process is repeated until water covers the top
of the model. The water is then poured out of the tank,
leaving the coast with lines marked on it at regular intervals
above and below high water mark. The children see that the
lines are drawn at regular intervals to represent height.
Furthermore they are drawn on smooth or even slopes and do not
represent sudden steps or breaks in slope.

A sheet of thick acetate, as used on an overhead projector,
is now placed on top of the tank. By looking immediately over
the tank, the lines observed on the model are transferred with
a fibre tip pen on to the acetate (Figure 4.2). This is then
placed on the overhead projector and the pupils see a representation of a three-dimensional model in two-dimensional
form. In other words, the model has been transformed into a
map.

The lines are subsequently defined as contours and it is
essential that accurate terminology is used. The recommended
definition of a contour is 'a line drawn on a map through all

points which are at the same height above, or depth below, sea level'. This definition draws attention to the fact that contours are lines drawn on maps and do not appear on the ground. It is also a reminder that they can be drawn above or below sea level. This is important in view of the inclusion of submarine contours both on Ordnance Survey maps of coastal areas and on atlas maps.

The value of engaging children in practical activity when they are learning to read maps has already been stressed and it is probably nowhere more important than in developing the concept of contours. Each pair of children in the class should be provided with a small piece of plasticine with which to mould their own stretch of coastline. This can be placed in any small container with a flat base and open top such as a polythene sandwich box. The children then pour water from milk bottles into their boxes and mark on the rising water levels with a ball point pen. When they have marked on five or six levels they pour the water into a bucket and place a piece of acetate over the top of the box. They then look down on the box and trace the contour lines from the model. The children should write an account of the experiment, illustrating it with their own diagram of their model and concluding it with the contour tracing made from the model. If the definition of a contour is provided by the teacher all of the remaining writing can be in the children's own words.

The concept of contours may be further reinforced with another exercise on the plasticine model. It can be cut into horizontal sections along the line of each contour. Each section is laid in turn on a sheet of acetate, the contour outline is drawn round it, and the area within it is coloured. In this way a contour map is built up and the end result is a map with layer shading. The children can do the same with their own models, using plain paper for drawing the contours and crayons to colour the area enclosed by each contour.

The way in which steep and gentle slopes are shown as contour patterns can be demonstrated with a similar model, but on this occasion the central section of coastline is made of sand and only the edges are made of plasticine. The tank is one-third filled with water and a short piece of wood is then moved to and fro in the water to simulate wave action. After a few minutes a bay will be formed in the sand, bounded by headlands on each side in the plasticine. This not only illustrates processes of wave action at work but produces landforms from which contours patterns can be traced. The steep slopes of the headlands and more gentle slopes of the bay will be reflected respectively in closely spaced and widely spaced contour lines.

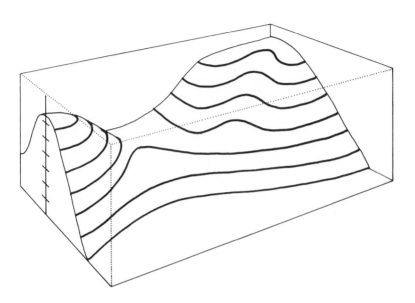

FIGURE 4.1. CONTOURS ON A MODEL IN A TANK

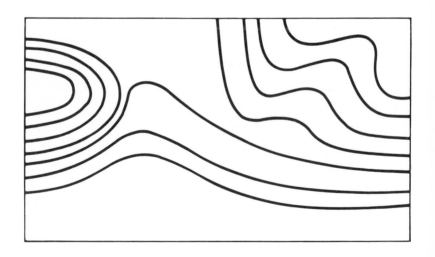

FIGURE 4.2. CONTOUR MAP OF THE MODEL

The same model can be used to demonstrate the formation of river valleys and the associated contour patterns. Layers of plasticine are again placed on each side of the central area of sand. On this occasion, however, water is poured very slowly from the back of the tank on to the sand. Within a few minutes the water will form a valley in the sand and collect at the foot of the sand to form a coastline. The resulting contour pattern can be seen after removing the water.

The plasticene can likewise be used to illustrate hill contour patterns. The parts nearest the coast will form headlands projecting out into the sea. Further inland these ridges can be moulded to rise to small hills with enclosed contours. Again the contour patterns associated with these two types of landforms can be seen from the model. It will be readily apparent that other types of landform, such as a col, spur, plateau and escarpment, can be moulded in plasticine. In each case the contour pattern can be clearly observed. The procedure will help to overcome the tendency of some pupils to visualise rivers as flowing along spurs instead of down valleys. In such cases they have simply associated the words 'spur' and 'valley' with a visual pattern of contours rather than with the slopes that the pattern represents.

Landscape Models

When the children understand the concept of contours they should construct a layer model from contour patterns shown on a map. This should be a map of an area of gentle relief, such as that of the school neighbourhood, local park or some other area with which the children are familiar. The largest scale Ordnance Survey map on which contours are shown is the 1:10,000 series and its predecessor the 1:10,560 (6 inches to 1 mile) series. The whole country, both urban and rural areas, is covered by the series. A small part of the map is enlarged two or three times by copying the contours on to bigger squares on a large sheet of paper. Alternatively an overhead projector transparency can be made by heat copying process and then projected on to a large sheet of paper pinned to a wall, on to which the contours are transferred (Figure 4.3).

Expanded polystyrene ceiling tiles measuring 30 cm by 30 cm (12 in by 12 in) form ideal material for making a layer model, as they are light, cheap and easily cut with a sharp knife. A strong hardboard or plywood base the same size as the enlarged map is needed and this is covered with a layer of tiles. The enlarged map is placed on top of this layer of tiles and the lowest two contours are transferred to the tiles by punching lines of holes through the paper with any pointed instrument such as a sharp pencil. The map is then removed and the lower of the two contours is cut out with a knife, the higher contour remaining as a marker for the next one. The map is placed in position again and the process is repeated, the next layer of tiles being correctly aligned with the marker on the layer below. Successive tiles are glued in position until the highest contour is reached and the layer model is complete. Figure 4.4 shows a layer model constructed from the contour lines on the map in Figure 4.3. The model measures 60 cm by 60 cm (24 in by 24 in), four tiles being joined together as the base to form the lowest layer.

It is most important that the model is not left in this form because the stepped or terraced appearance bears no resemblance to the real landscape. The spaces between the layers should be filled in with tightly screwed paper and covered with plaster or filler, which is smoothed out so that the final appearance of the model is similar to the relief of the landscape represented on the map. The model is then painted and selected features placed on it in their correct locations. Figure 4.5 shows the completed model of the land shown on the map in Figure 4.3. It is painted green, the rivers being added in blue and the lanes in black. Pieces of matchstick painted red represent buildings.

The whole purpose of building a relief model is to help children to visualise the landscape from the contour map. For this reason care should be taken to avoid the excessive exaggeration of relief which occurs if very thick tiles or other layers of material are used in building the model. Vertical exaggeration is rarely given adequate attention in model building with the result that children may easily develop a distorted impression of a landscape. They should work out the vertical exaggeration of the model as an extension of their work in mathematics. On a 1:10,000 map, 1 cm represents 10,000 cm or 100 m on the ground. This means that the vertical scale would also have to be 1 cm to 100 m if the model is to be an exact replica of the landscape. In other words, if card 1 mm thick is used to represent each 10 m in height, there will be no vertical exaggeration. In practice this would be insufficient to bring out the differences between the lower and higher parts of an area of gentle relief. If the difference in height is 100 m, the model would be only 1 cm high. Thus it is generally advisable to use thicker material. If card 2 mm thick is used to represent each 10 m in height, for example, the vertical exaggeration is x2. Similarly 3 mm to 10 m gives a vertical exaggeration x3, 4 mm gives x4 and 5 mm gives x5. The latter is usually regarded as the maximum desirable if distorted impressions of landscapes are to be avoided.

Contours are shown at intervals of 25 feet on 1:10,560 maps and, for the purpose of calculating vertical exaggeration on models, this may be regarded as an interval of approximately 8 metres. The scale of the map used as the basis of the model shown in Figure 4.5 becomes approximately 1:3,550 after enlargement. Each polystyrene tile is 6 mm thick and represents an increase in height of 25 feet or about 8 metres. Hence 6 mm on the model represents 8,000 mm on the ground, which gives a vertical scale of about 1:1,333. Thus the vertical exaggeration is approximately x2½.

A model is valuable in helping pupils to understand the concept of a cross section, which is most easily described as a slice through the landscape. The side of a relief model is, in effect, a section across the landscape. It is helpful for children to begin by drawing a section across a large scale map of an area for which they have previously constructed a model. They will then see that the section simply shows in two dimensions what the model shows in three dimensions.

The line of the section should be drawn on the map to avoid errors. The straight edge of a piece of paper is placed along the section line. Each point at which a contour meets the edge of the paper is marked on it and numbered. When two adjacent contours have the same number care must be taken to indicate with a plus or minus sign whether the land between them rises or falls. The piece of paper is then placed along a base line drawn on squared paper. The heights recorded are transferred as a series of dots at the corresponding heights on the vertical scale. The dots are subsequently joined by means of a smooth curve. The positions of prominent features can be indicated by means of labelled arrows, the scale and vertical exaggeration should be stated, and the grid references and direction of the section should be indicated at each end of it. Figure 4.6 shows a section drawn from the south-west corner to the north-east corner of the map (Figure 4.3) used as the base for the landscape model (Figure 4.5), and illustrates the distorting effect of vertical exaggeration.

As with models, the choice of a vertical scale in drawing sections should not be so great that it results in an excessive exaggeration of relief. Gently rolling hill and vale countryside can quickly be transformed into mountainous scenery in this way, thus giving a totally distorted impression of landscape. Children should always work out the vertical exaggeration and state it on the section. Calculations should be given in full and the reasoning should be clear. Care should be taken to use the same imperial or metric units on the vertical scale as on the horizontal scale and this is ensured if each one is given as a ratio. The ratio 1:10,000

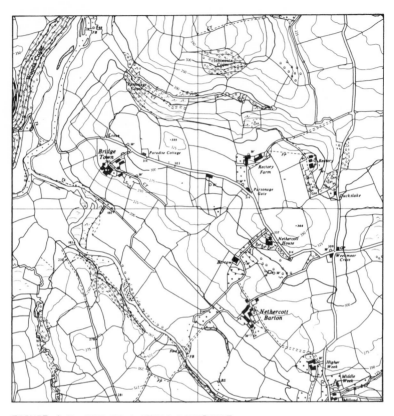

FIGURE 4.3. MAP OF A DEVON LANDSCAPE

THE THIRD DIMENSION

FIGURE 4.4. LANDSCAPE MODEL UNDER CONSTRUCTION

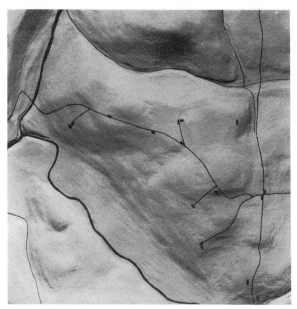

FIGURE 4.5. LANDSCAPE MODEL AFTER COMPLETION

THE THIRD DIMENSION

A: No exageration. B: Exaggeration x3. C: Exaggeration x6.

FIGURE 4.6. THE EFFECT OF VERTICAL EXAGGERATION

68

or 1:10,560 simply means that one inch on the map or section represents 10,000 or 1:10,560 inches on the ground. If the vertical scale chosen is 1 inch to 200 feet, this is a ratio of 1:200 x12 or 1:2,400. The vertical exaggeration, there-- fore, is slightly more than x4. As a general rule an exag- geration x5 should be regarded as the maximum.

When children are drawing sections for the first time they will find it helpful to colour the base map carefully to show the changes in height. All land between two successive contours should be shaded in the same colour and the sequence of colours should be carefully chosen so that lighter shades represent the lower land and darker shades the higher land. Colouring or layer shading the base map in this way will help children to distinguish contour lines from other details on the map, such as streams and field boundaries. If the same sequence of colours is then used on the completed section, children can compare the map and section more readily. They will see that the layer shading on the map simply indicates land on a continuous slope between specified heights, and that a change in colour does not mean a sudden break in slope.

Children should then examine maps which employ layer tinting or the use of colours to show height intervals. The Ordnance Survey 1:63,360 (1 inch to 1 mile) tourist maps covering selected parts of the country which are popular for recreational purposes use colours as well as contours to show relief. The lowland areas (below 700 feet) are coloured with a pale green wash, land intermediate in height (between 700 and 1300 feet) in three shades of yellow, and the higher land (above 1300 feet) in three shades of brown. The layer tinting on these tourist maps enables the reader to distinguish upland from lowland areas much more readily than on 1:25,000 and 1:50,000 maps which use contours alone. The additional use of grey hill shading on the tourist maps is also effective in creating a three-dimensional impression of relief, particularly in highland areas such as the English Lake District. A similar sequence of layer tinting together with hill shading is used on 1:250,000 (4 inches to 1 mile) maps.

Relief is a conspicuous feature of most atlas maps other than those showing purely political boundaries. The well known colour scheme of green for lowland, yellows and browns for higher land, and sometimes reds for the highest mountainous areas, is purely conventional and not derived from any particular sequence of colours in the spectrum. An inter- national commission adopted the sequence when planning a series of 1:1,000,000 maps covering the world. Psychological studies have not shown any relationship, however, between this sequence of colours and the ability to perceive changes of height on maps (Bartz, 1970). Yet the information presented through these colours dominates the image of the world that children acquire from studying atlas maps. The colours can lead to completely distorted images, such as the association of green with meadow and the interpretation of a series of altitude tints to indicate land rising like a flight of stairs (Sandford, 1972). Errors of this kind arise from failure to read and understand the key to the map, so it is important that children are taught to refer to the map key to explain the correct meaning of colours.

The addition of hill shading to conventional atlas maps to create a more vivid impression of mountains and valleys does not always have the desired effect. Sometimes the resulting image of landscape that children acquire is quite different from that intended (Sandford, 1978). Much depends on the manner in which the hill shading is done. It can be produced in various ways, such as by applying an air brush or photographing a relief model, but it requires considerable skill to be effective.

Satellite photography can now be used to produce atlas maps and is employed in Bartholomew's series of atlases of the environment. The main types of vegetation appear in their natural colours, forests being shown in green and deserts in brown, whilst cultivated land is given the yellow colour of ripe grain. Hill shading is added to produce a realistic three-dimensional view of the world as seen from space. Environmental maps are thus designed to avoid the misleading impressions of fertile deserts and mountains rising above plains like flights of stairs which are conveyed by the altitude tints of conventional atlas maps.

Landscape models can be used to test children's concepts of projective space by following the procedure employed by Piaget in the three mountains experiment described in Chapter 1. The construction of models may take up a considerable amount of time but this is necessary if children are to acquire a true understanding of the landscape represented by contours and avoid the misconceptions noted by Boardman and Towner (1979) and discussed in Chapter 2. Attempts to teach three-dimensional concepts solely from two-dimensional documents are unlikely to be successful with many children. It is difficult enough for children to think and visualise in three-dimensional space, but it is even more difficult for them to do so when they can only see three-dimensional ideas represented in a distorted two-dimensional manner on paper.

Practical activities with materials should have a place in most subjects of the curriculum according to Eggleston (1976), who urges consultation between craft, design and

technology departments and those in other subjects. Col-
laboration between geography teachers and craft and design
teachers has also been recommended by Boardman (1982a) in
arguing the case for the construction of landscape models as
a means of developing graphicacy. A report from the Design
Council (1980) has likewise advocated interdisciplinary work
with materials, especially where it helps to develop children's understanding of, and responsibility towards, the
environment in which they live.

Landscape Sketches

The sketching of landscapes is an important means of helping
children not only to understand the third dimension of the
landscape but also to record it on paper. Landscape sketching is a standard method of recording in the field yet has
been described as a neglected aspect of graphicacy (Simmons
and Mears, 1977). The advantage of sketching is that it
demands careful observation and close attention to detail.
Since primary, middle and lower secondary school children
often display these abilities it is appropriate to give them
opportunities to draw sketches.

The difficulties which many children experience with
this form of drawing, however, should not be underestimated.
A basic problem is that of co-ordination. Children have to
recognise the boundaries of the area to be sketched and
determine the features of the landscape to be drawn. They
have to show the main lines which form the basic features
and then keep looking at these features whilst transferring
the images to lines on paper. In addition the complication
of perspective affects all three-dimensional drawing. Clearly
considerable benefits can be gained from seeking the guidance
of art teachers in a school. Indeed graphicacy has been
discussed as one of six rationales for art education by
Barrett (1979).

Methods of landscape sketching are best introduced and
practised in the classroom before outdoor work is attempted.
A simple but effective method of sketching from a photograph
is to project a 35 mm transparency mounted as a slide first
on to a screen and then on to a blackboard. Whilst the slide
is projected on to the screen the important features on it
are brought to the attention of the class. When the slide
is projected on to the blackboard the teacher traces the outline of the image with chalk. The slide projector is then
switched off, leaving the outline on the blackboard so that
the important features can be arrowed and labelled by the
teacher. The slide can be projected on to the screen a
second time if desired so that these features can be seen
again by the class, or alternatively slide and sketch can be

FIGURE 4.7. PHOTOGRAPH ALONG SECTION LINE

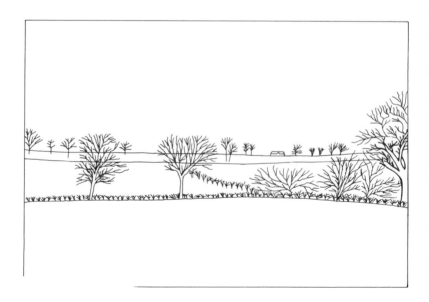

FIGURE 4.8. SKETCH DRAWN FROM PHOTOGRAPH

viewed simultaneously for comparison.

The technique of drawing on the blackboard whilst the class watches is valuable in that the children can follow the construction of the outline. The teacher should stress the need for a simple but clear outline of the main features of a landscape scene and illustrate the principles of perspective. Alternatively the outline can be drawn beforehand on an over-head transparency by projecting the slide on to a sheet of white paper pinned to a wall, the projector being brought close to the wall to reduce the size of image. The outline can then be drawn in the same way as on the blackboard, thus providing a permanent record of the main features of the picture. A similar method can be used to transfer the photograph on to a piece of A4 size paper, which can then easily be duplicated in quantities by normal spirit or ink duplicating process, all children in the class being given copies to label.

An example of a photograph used in this way is il-lustrated in Figure 4.7. The photograph covers part of the area shown on the landscape model (Figure 4.5). It was taken from a point near the river on the line of the section (Figure 4.6), with the camera pointing towards the north-east. An outline sketch drawn from the photograph is shown in Figure 4.8. Children should compare the map with the sketch and photograph in order to see the effects of per-spective, particularly on distance. Although features in the foreground are large because of proximity to the camera, the distance from left to right is short, only a few metres im-mediately in front of the camera. The distance from left to right increases with distance from the camera until on the skyline in the background it is nearly 400 metres. Children can also measure the distance from foreground to background by locating these on the map and calculating the real distance with the aid of the scale. The advantage of using a photograph, sketch and map of an area for which a land-scape model has been constructed will be apparent.

Work in the classroom should be a prelude to, and training for, the freehand drawing of landscape sketches out of doors. For the first attempt the teacher may wish to provide an outline sketch which the children annotate in the way which has already been described. The children then relate the sketch and map to the real landscape. Subsequently they should attempt to draw their own freehand sketches, but they may need considerable help in the early stages.

A useful aid for sketching in the field is a sketching frame, which consists of a rectangular frame constructed from wood or thick card and thus resembles a picture frame.

Its purpose is to concentrate the child's attention on the features of the landscape which appear inside the frame and to exclude those outside it. The size of the frame can vary from that of a postcard to that of a sheet of A4 paper, depending upon the extent of the landscape to be sketched and the distance the child stands or sits behind the frame. The inside of the frame can be crossed by a series of tightly stretched threads or by a number of thin lines drawn on a sheet of acetate placed over the frame. This grid conveniently divides the area into squares and helps the child to maintain accuracy whilst drawing the landscape on a sheet of paper similarly divided up into squares and mounted on a drawing board or other hard surface. The sketching frame is held in position by fixing it to a ranging pole or other piece of timber which is then driven into the ground. If a short pole is used the child can remain seated whilst drawing the sketch. When the child has had some practice in sketching in this way, the grid can be removed from the frame whilst a further sketch is attempted. Eventually the frame is discarded so that the child has to draw a landscape unaided. Further advice about landscape drawing is contained in the classic volume by Hutchings (1960) and various other techniques are described by Simmons and Mears (1977).

The principles of field sketching apply equally to the urban environments in which most children live. Sketching of urban landscapes may begin at ground level with a single building in the school neighbourhood in order to encourage detailed scrutiny of its constituent parts. Alternatively a group of buildings, such as a row of terraced houses or shops, may be sketched and labelled, ages estimated and building materials noted. If it is possible to gain access to a high vantage point, such as the top of a tall block of flats, skyline sketching may be attempted. This involves the sketching of a panorama of buildings of different sizes, shapes and heights, such as those found near to the centre of most towns. Younger, inexperienced or less able pupils may find this a rather difficult task and it will be advisable for the teacher to prepare an outline sketch, if necessary drawn from a photograph taken from the viewpoint. It is important that outline sketches are accurate, with individual buildings correctly positioned and clearly drawn. Urban landscapes are often very complex to analyse, even though children may be familiar with their components through everyday experience.

Aerial Photographs

The correlation of aerial photographs with Ordnance Survey maps is a demanding task for children to attempt and gives rise to numerous difficulties. Exercises of this kind involve children in the mental processes necessary for transforming

the three-dimensional townscape, through the intermediate
stage of the oblique aerial photograph, to the final vertical
representation on the map. The task of matching details on an
aerial photograph with those on a map requires not only the
ability to recognise the features in an unfamiliar form but
also to conserve mentally their correct spatial arrangement.
Children tend to assume that the top of a photograph is north
irrespective of the direction in which the camera is pointing
when a photograph is taken. They also tend to overestimate
the size of the area shown on a photograph when they compare
it with the map (Boardman and Towner, 1980).

        Aerial photographs of the area around a school are some-
times difficult to obtain. The main national suppliers such
as Aerofilms have a comprehensive coverage of rural areas and
the central parts of towns and cities, but this does not
always extend to the suburbs in which most schools are situated.
There are also problems of copyright, payment of royalties and
expense of reproduction when class sets of photographs are
required. It is worth making enquiries at local photographic
studios, particularly newspaper offices, for good low level
oblique aerial photographs. Such studios are often willing to
enlarge small negatives to A4 size black and white prints and
to produce multiple copies by offset-litho press at moderate
cost. If studios retain the negatives it is not normally
necessary to purchase the copyright or to make royalty pay-
ments.

        Children may need considerable help when they attempt to
orientate an oblique aerial photograph with an Ordnance Survey
map for the first time. It will be advisable to start with a
photograph of the local area in which the camera is pointing
north, north-east, or north-west. This will mean that the
children will be able to orientate map and photograph more
easily and it will be unnecessary for them to keep turning the
map round in order to read names on it. An arrow can be drawn
on the map to show the direction on which the camera is pointing. Subsequently children can examine photographs in which
the camera is pointing west, east or south so that they become
accustomed to the idea of orientating a map with a photograph.

        The similarity of the shapes of map and photograph, which
are both usually rectangular or square, can be misleading.
Because of the effects of perspective, the area shown on an
oblique aerial photograph is no longer square or rectangular
when transferred to the map. Neither is it necessarily
triangular nor the shape of a trapezium, for even the edges
may be curved rather than straight. Initially it will be
advisable to delimit carefully on the map the edges of the
area shown on the photograph.

Differences between the scale of a map, which is constant over the whole of a map, and the scale of a photograph, which varies with distance from the camera, needs to be drawn to the children's attention. Once the boundaries of the area shown on the photograph have been drawn on the map, the children can measure the distance across the foreground, middle-ground and background of the photograph. They can also measure the distance from the foreground to the background. Comparison between photograph and map will also help them to visualise what distances measured on the map are actually like on the ground.

The distorting effect of perspective on the size of individual features also needs to be considered. Features such as buildings in the foreground of a photograph tend to be overemphasised whilst those of similar size in the background tend to be underemphasised. The size of features in the foreground and background of a map should be compared with their size on a large scale map. It is equally important to do so if a smaller scale map is being used, when certain features are shown by means of symbols. The amount of space taken up by the symbol for a church, for example, can be compared with the small amount of space the church occupies on a photograph.

An outline drawing of an oblique aerial photograph is a useful aid when children are comparing it with a map. It is advisable to begin with a photograph of the area around the school, such as that around St. Mary's R.C. Primary School in the Birmingham suburb of Harborne shown in Figure 4.9. The corresponding area on the Ordnance Survey map is shown in Figure 4.10. It will be noted that the camera was pointing towards the north-east when the photograph was taken and so the orientation is only slightly different from that of the map itself. The viewpoint and direction can be indicated on the map to assist with orientation.

The edges of the map are shown by lines on an outline drawing which is prepared by placing tracing paper over the photograph and drawing prominent features on it (Figure 4.11). In this case the main roads are labelled 1 to 4 (High Street, Harborne Park Road, Vivian Road and Greenfield Road), four large buildings are labelled A to D (the school, the church, the social club and a garage), together with two areas of open space, X (bowling green), and Y (school playground). The children have to identify these ten features by using the out-line drawing in conjunction with the photograph and comparing both with the map. The slight distortion of the road pattern and differences in the size of buildings on the photograph will be noted.

Subsequently children can attempt to correlate oblique aerial photographs with maps on ever-decreasing scales. Maps on the 1:10,000 and 1:10,560 scales are useful for this purpose, but photographs will usually have to be taken from higher altitudes in order to cover larger areas. In any case it is instructive for children to note the reduction in detail which results from the representation of an entire 1:2,500 map as only one of 25 grid squares on a 1:10,000 map. Orientation of map and photograph can be made more difficult if the camera is pointing towards the west or east instead of north. A south orientation, however, is best avoided because children have to keep turning the map round in order to read off names from it.

Care should be taken if there is a difference of several years between the dates of the printing of photograph and map, especially in urban areas where demolition and redevelopment may have taken place. If this has occurred, children can search for differences in the detail shown by map and photograph. When comparing the map (Figure 4.10) with the photograph (Figure 4.9) it will be seen that in Harborne Park Road, for example, the houses next to the public house have been demolished and a church has been built on the nearby plot of vacant land.

The correlation of oblique aerial photographs taken from higher altitudes with 1:25,000 and 1:50,000 maps is more difficult because of further reduction in the detail shown on photographs of extensive areas and the use of symbolism for many features on these smaller scale maps. Pupils may require assistance in orientating the photograph and map, particularly if the camera was pointing towards the east, west or south. The attention of pupils needs to be drawn to the considerable differences in scale between map and photograph, and they may require help in comparing distances on the two documents. The distorting effect of the perspective of the photograph has to he continually emphasised until it is fully appreciated.

FIGURE 4.9. AERIAL PHOTOGRAPH OF HARBORNE. Graveley of Birmingham

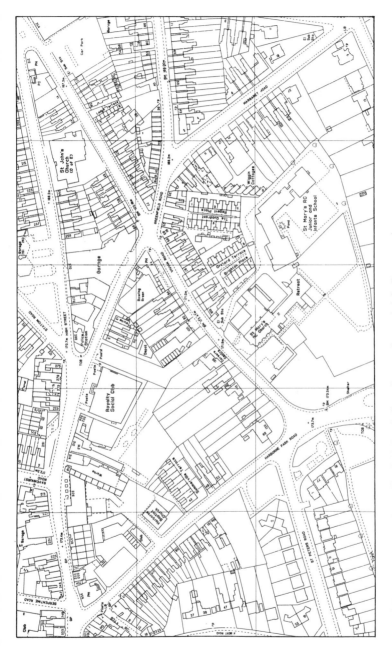

FIGURE 4.10. MAP OF PART OF HARBORNE. Crown Copyright Reserved

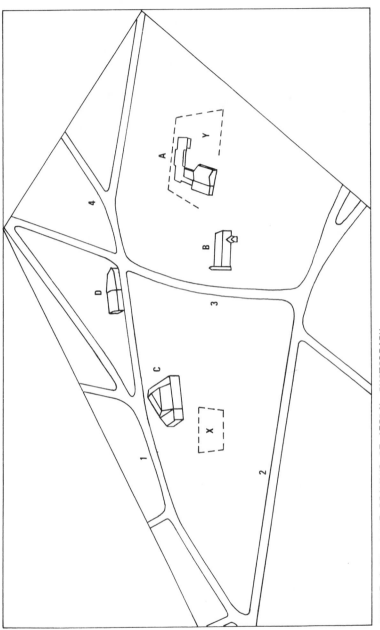

FIGURE 4.11. LINE DRAWING OF AERIAL PHOTOGRAPH

5 Examination Courses

Geography is a subject taken by about half of the pupils in the
fourth and fifth years of secondary schools. It attracts
large numbers of subject entries in public examinations, both
in the General Certificate of Education (GCE) at Ordinary
Level, which is designed for pupils in the top 20 per cent of
the ability range, and in the Certificate of Secondary
Education (CSE), which is intended for the next 40 per cent
of the ability range. This chapter examines the role of work
with Ordnance Survey maps and photographs in developing
graphicacy in pupils during their last two years of statutory
education. The analysis covers both conventional O-level and
CSE courses and also those initiated by two Schools Council
geography projects. An approach to map reading and interpretation based on intensive, in-depth study of an area is
advocated in order to assist the pupils' visualisation and
comprehension of the landscape depicted on 1:25,000 and
1:50,000 scale maps.

CSE and O-level

All thirteen of the CSE examinations boards in England and
Wales include Ordnance Survey map reading in their Mode 1
syllabuses. Eleven boards set a compulsory question on it
and this is usually the only compulsory question on the examination paper, although some boards also have a compulsory
question on atlas map reading, or a series of objective-type
questions sampling a large section of the geography syllabus.
Whilst most boards state that candidates should be familiar
with maps on both the 1:25,000 and the 1:50,000 scales, some
specify that only those on a scale of 1:50,000 will be used
in the examination. A few boards provide key sheets of conventional signs for use in the examination but most expect
candidates to know the symbols.

Indeed there is some variation in the amount of detail
on map reading which is provided in the syllabuses of the CSE
boards. The West Midlands Board, for example, states briefly
that: 'The first question will be compulsory and will involve
the interpretation of an Ordnance Survey map (1:50,000 or
1:25,000 scales). Centres must supply candidates with the OS
symbols key for use in the examination'. The East Midlands
Board provides somewhat more detail: 'A map extract on either
1:50,000 or 1:25,000 scale will be used and a key to the
symbols will be provided. Questions will be confined to the
area of the extract which may be from anywhere in the British
Isles except the East Midlands. The questions will be framed
to test knowledge of geographical grammar (grid references,
scale, distance, direction, simple contour patterns) and the
simple interpretation of the physical and human geography of
the area'. Both of these boards offer alternative syllabuses:
'a conceptual approach to the study of geography'(West
Midlands) and one which includes 'some of the many new developments in geography in a realistic form suitable for CSE pupils'
(East Midlands). In neither of these is Ordnance Survey map
reading compulsory, although the use of maps is encouraged.

Most boards expect candidates to be able to recognise
conventional signs or symbols, without necessarily memorising
them, to use grid references, to measure distances and to
state directions. Candidates are also expected to read heights
and recognise simple contour patterns and gradients, although
they are not normally required to calculate gradients. The
Southern Board expects candidates to determine the inter-
visibility of points by means of an accurate section. The
South East Board, however, specifically states that candidates
will not be expected to draw cross sections or work out
gradients, although they may be required to comment on given
cross sections and asked to assess the relative merits of the
varied gradients of alternative routes shown on the map. The
Welsh Board gives examples of the simple landforms which candidates should know, such as valley, steep slope, spur,
plateau, gap and cliff. Some boards specify that a photograph
of part of the area shown on the map may be provided for use
in conjunction with the map during the examination. Two
boards give advice on the kinds of landscapes which will be
represented on the map used in the examination. The South
Western Board specifies a coastal area, a chalk area, a limestone area or a glaciated highland area. The West Yorkshire
and Lindsey Board states that the types of area from which the
map will be selected are chalk or limestone and clay areas,
glaciated areas, highlands and lowlands, industrial areas and
coastal areas.

An analysis of the Ordnance Survey map reading questions set in CSE Mode 1 examination papers in 1980 is given in Table 5.1. The types of questions are divided into three categories: reading and calculation, transformation and interpretation. Reading and calculation includes symbols located by means of grid references, together with statements of distance, direction, height and gradient. All of these skills receive considerable emphasis in CSE examinations. Location questions usually require the use of grid references to identify a specific symbol, for which a key is rarely provided. Presumably candidates are expected to memorise all of the symbols on 1:25,000 and 1:50,000 maps! Questions on distance, which are often linked to direction, normally involve straight-line measurement on the map and conversion using the scale provided. The reading of height from the map normally involves the identification of a spot height or a specific contour. Calculation of gradient when required is usually based on the distance between two spot heights.

The second category, transformation, requires candidates to transfer information on the map into another form, such as a cross section or profile, a sketch map on the same or a reduced scale, or a landscape sketch based on a photograph. The candidates are usually required to identify specific features on the photograph with the corresponding features on the map, to show that they have managed to orientate and cor-relate the two documents. Candidates may be asked to annotate an outline sketch map of the area or to insert in the correct locations on the outline map certain specified features. Alternatively they may be asked to make use of a cross section to help them to indicate ways in which the routes taken by a road and a railway differ from each other.

The third category, interpretation, although tested by all boards, constitutes a much smaller component than each of the previous two categories. Candidates are sometimes asked to describe the relief and drainage in a specified part of the map, or to show how relief and drainage change along a particular grid line. Questions on communications usually ask candidates to describe and give reasons for the pattern of main routes on the map. Settlement questions are usually concerned with the site and situation of a town or number of villages. Map interpretation draws many comments from examiners in their reports. The following are examples from reports on the 1980 examination: 'Many candidates are still unable to interpret simple contour patterns' (West Midlands Board). 'Candidates should realise that contours are not a feature of the landscape' (East Midlands Board). 'Large numbers of candidates are not learning basic map skills and very few can read contours ' (London Board).

TABLE 5.1 C.S.E. MAP READING QUESTIONS 1980

Exam Board	READING AND CALCULATION							TRANSFORMATION			INTERPRETATION					
	Location	Symbols	Distance	Direction	Height	Gradient	Photograph Orientation	Landscape Sketch	Sketch Map Annotation	Cross Section Annotation	Relief and Drainage	Settlement	Communications	Comparison of Two Areas	Pattern of Distribution	Human Activity in Relation to Physical Environment
South Western Exam Board	1	1	1	1	1	0	1	0	0	0	1	1	1	0	0	1
Southern Regional Exam Board	1	1	1	1	0	0	1	0	0	0	0	1	1	0	1	1
South East Regional Exam Board	1	0	0	1	0	0	1	0	0	1	1	0	0	0	0	1
London Regional Exam Board	1	1	1	1	1	0	1	0	1	1	0	1	0	0	0	0
East Anglian Exam Board (N)	1	1	1	0	0	0	0	0	1	1	0	0	1	0	0	1
East Anglian Exam Board (S)	1	1	1	1	1	0	1	0	0	0	0	1	1	0	0	0
East Midlands Regional Exam Board (Syllabus 1)	1	0	0	1	0	0	1	0	0	0	1	1	1	0	0	0
West Midlands Regional Exam Board (Syllabus A)	1	1	0	0	0	0	0	0	0	0	0	1	1	0	0	0
North West Regional Exam Board	1	1	1	1	0	0	1	0	0	0	1	1	1	0	0	0
Associated Lancashire Schools Exam Board	0	1	0	1	0	0	0	0	0	0	0	1	1	1	1	0
West Yorks & Lindsey Exam Board	1	1	1	1	1	1	1	0	0	0	1	0	0	0	0	0
Yorkshire Regional Exam Board	1	1	1	1	1	0	0	1	0	0	0	1	1	0	0	0
North Regional Education Board	1	1	0	1	1	0	1	0	0	0	1	1	1	0	0	0
Welsh Joint Education Committee	0	1	1	0	1	0	0	0	1	0	1	1	1	0	0	0

EXAMINATION COURSES

All eight of the GCE examinations boards in England and Wales attach importance to the candidates' ability to read and interpret Ordnance Survey maps on scales of 1:25,000 and 1:50,000 in the Ordinary Level examination. All boards include Ordnance Survey map reading and interpretation in their O-level syllabuses and all of them set a compulsory question on it in their examinations. Indeed it is the only compulsory question set in O-level geography papers.

There is considerable variation, however, in the amount of detail which is provided in O-level syllabuses. The briefest statements are to be found in the syllabus of the Joint Matriculation Board, which simply states 'the elements of map reading (Ordnance Survey 1:50,000 and 1:25,000 maps)' and in the syllabus of the Oxford and Cambridge Board, which equally briefly states 'the ability to interpret Ordnance Survey maps on the scales of 1:50,000 and 1:25,000'. The Cambridge Board, however, specifies in its syllabus the types of detailed questions which may be set, including grid references, conventional signs, gradients, measurement of distance, orientation, and methods of representing scale, as well as the description and patterns of relief, drainage, settlement and communications. In the alternative syllabus offered by the Cambridge Board candidates may use the Ordnance Survey map to answer several questions, although none is compulsory. Alone among the boards, London provides a key to conventional signs for all Ordnance Survey map questions in the examination, thus eliminating the need for candidates to memorise the symbols, a requirement of all other boards. London also offers two syllabuses at O-level (A and B) and, although the Ordnance Survey map used is the same in both examinations, the questions set are different.

Two boards devote the whole of one examination paper to Ordnance Survey map reading and interpretation. The Southern Universities Joint Board sets a one-hour paper, the syllabus for which is the use and interpretation of topographical maps, and also of additional material such as photographs, diagrams and statistical information which would facilitate the inter- pretation and understanding of the maps. The Associated Examining Board sets a 45-minute paper on map reading and interpretation. The syllabus lists the techniques which may be tested and the interpretation of information which will be expected. It also specifies the comparison between a photo- graph and a map of the same area.

An analysis of the O-level Ordnance Survey map reading questions set by the eight GCE boards in 1980 is provided in Table 5.2. The same three categories of questions as for CSE are used in the table: reading and calculation, transformation and interpretation. It will be seen that reading and calcula-

TABLE 5.2 G.C.E. O-LEVEL MAP READING QUESTIONS 1980

	READING AND CALCULATION						TRANSFORMATION				INTERPRETATION					
	Location	Symbols	Distance	Direction	Height	Gradient	Photograph Orientation	Landscape Sketch	Sketch Map Annotation	Cross Section Annotation	Relief and Drainage	Settlement	Communications	Comparison of Two Areas	Pattern of Distribution	Human Activity in Relation to Physical Environment
Associated Examining Board	0	0	0	0	1	0	1	1	0	0	1	1	1	1	0	1
Joint Matriculation Board	0	0	0	0	0	1	0	0	0	0	1	1	1	1	0	1
Oxford & Cambridge Schools Exam Board	1	1	1	1	1	0	1	1	0	1	1	1	0	0	0	1
Oxford Delegacy of Local Exams	0	0	0	0	0	0	0	0	0	0	1	0	0	0	1	1
Southern Universities Joint Board	0	0	0	0	0	0	0	0	0	0	1	1	1	1	1	1
University of Cambridge Local Exam Syndicate (1)	1	0	0	0	0	1	1	0	0	0	1	1	0	0	0	1
University of Cambridge Local Exam Syndicate (2)	0	0	0	0	0	0	0	0	0	0	1	1	1	0	0	1
University of London Examinations Board (A)	0	0	0	0	0	0	0	0	1	1	1	1	0	0	1	1
University of London Examinations Board (B)	1	1	0	0	0	1	0	0	0	0	1	1	1	0	0	1
Welsh Joint Education Committee	0	0	0	0	0	0	0	0	1	0	1	1	1	1	0	1
Geography 14-18 Project	0	0	0	0	0	0	0	0	1	1	1	1	1	1	1	1
Avery Hill 14-16 Project	0	1	0	0	0	0	0	0	0	0	0	1	1	0	0	1

tion play a much smaller role in O-level papers than in CSE papers. The second category, transformation, receives a similar amount of attention in both O-level and CSE examinations. It is the third category, interpretation, which is given a great deal more emphasis at O-level than at CSE. All GCE boards set questions on relief and drainage, and on human activity in relation to the physical environment. Most also include questions on settlement and communications, and some on patterns of distribution, or the comparison of two areas.

The interpretation questions set by different boards are similar. All boards expect candidates to be able to describe relief and drainage; often the question says no more than 'Describe the main features of the relief and drainage' in a specified part of the map. Questions on communications are frequently related to those on relief; the following is typical: 'Compare and contrast, in relation to relief, the route followed by the railway with that followed by the trunk road'. Settlement questions tend to be related in part to relief or communications: 'Describe the main features of the site, situation, form and functions of the town'. Candidates may be asked to compare and contrast two settlements or areas, or to describe the pattern of settlement or other distribution shown on the map. Sometimes a sketch map outline or grid on the same or a reduced scale may be provided, candidates having to add specific features to it. O-level candidates are nearly always expected to discuss some aspect of human activity in relation to the physical environment in which it occurs, as is appropriate for the more able pupils.

An indication of the kinds of difficulties experienced by candidates at O-level, however, is provided by the reports of examiners. Some boards are surprisingly unable to release these reports, regarding them as confidential to the schools which enter candidates for their examinations. Other boards produce reports which are so general and brief that they reveal little which is likely to be useful to teachers. Of the reports which are published, those produced by the Associated Examining Board and Joint Matriculation Board are by far the most detailed and informative. Reference to them will high-light some of the problems.

The correlation of a map with an oblique air photograph is required every year by the Associated Examining Board and reference is made almost annually to the difficulties which many candidates experience. Thus the task of combining the photograph and map to describe the features of a stretch of coastline 'proved relatively difficult and few candidates scored really well...errors were primarily ones of omission; it was common for descriptions to be undeveloped beyond the recognition of the cliff and the beach' (AEB, 1978). In the following year a question asked candidates to correlate a bridge on a photograph with one on the map, yet examiners estimated that as many as 50 per cent of the candidates gave the wrong answer to this question (AEB, 1979). A year later a photograph and sketch had to be orientated with a map of part of the Malvern Hills and Severn Valley and the examiners' report recognised that this was a demanding exercise. Commenting on this question, the report continued : 'Its design was built around a practical application of map reading skills, namely the problem facing a walker wishing to identify his/her position relative to the Ordnance Survey map and the view. Candidates whose preparation was limited to classroom analysis found the question more difficult than those who had experienced O S maps in the field. It is possible that some candidates who were unfamiliar with this type of exercise and did not appreciate the depth and perspective of the photograph spent a disproportionate amount of time answering the first part of the question' (AEB, 1980).

Interpretation of the physical landscape appears to present perplexing problems for many candidates. Thus one report observed that questions on relief and drainage had been set for several years, and yet candidates were often unable to give a clear description of the area represented on the map. 'Many candidates failed to recognise flat summits and ridge features, dissected by deep, narrow, steep-sided, winding, dry valleys, but switched on to "escarpment" and sought dip and scarp slopes all over the area' (JMB, 1978). The same report revealed that 'there was a quite alarming number of candidates who stated that rivers flow into the area from the sea'. Further errors concerning rivers were reported in the following year. 'There was almost universal misunderstanding of weirs and mill leats, which were referred to as, for example, "the river splits into two"... Many candidates wrote, incorrectly, in terms of tributaries that flow off from the main river, "it has many small rivers and streams leaving it"' (JMB, 1979). And from the next year's report: 'A matter of serious concern is the number of candidates who see the sources of streams as being points where streams go underground' (JMB, 1980). If these perceptual and conceptual problems are encountered by O-level candidates, they are likely to be experienced to an even greater degree by CSE candidates. An approach to teaching map interpretation to all pupils taking examination courses is discussed in the next section.

Map Interpretation

The interpretation of Ordnance Survey maps with examination classes builds on the pupils' achievements lower down the secondary school. It then progresses to work which should be

within the ability of most pupils following examination
courses in fourth and fifth forms, and concludes with exercises
which only the more able pupils may complete successfully.
The approach is based on the intensive, in-depth study of a
small area represented on a 1:25,000 or 1:50,000 Ordnance
Survey map extract of the kind used in public examinations.
The map should be carefully selected so as to provide contrasts
in relief and drainage. It should show both upland and lowland areas, and preferably exhibit landscapes developed on
differing rock types. The map should also show some settlements and communication links. The Edale-Castleton area of
Derbyshire fulfils these requirements and is used here for the
purposes of illustration.

Pupils begin by constructing a landscape model of the area
shown on the map using the procedure described in the previous
chapter. If the contours are closely spaced only the more
boldly drawn lines are traced off the map, such as the 100 foot
(30 metre) contours on a 1:25,000 map. On the Edale-Castleton
map (Figure 5.1) the land rises from a height of less than 600
feet in the south-east to nearly 2,000 feet in the north-west.
Pupils work in pairs to trace and transfer the fifteen 100
foot contours on to tiles, which they then cut to shape. The
model is built up as the tiles are placed in position on top
of each other, care being taken to ensure that closed contours,
such as the tops of hills or ridges, are accurately placed
using the successive sheets of tracing paper as guides. Once
glued securely, the steps between the tiles are smoothed out
with plaster. The model is given a coat of light green paint
and prominent features, such as the roads, railway and settlements, are painted on the model in distinctive colours. It
will be seen from drainage map (Figure 5.2) that the drainage
pattern of the Edale-Castleton area is complicated, and so
only the main two rivers are transferred to the model. The
construction of a landscape model of an area represented on an
Ordnance Survey map should be within the capabilities of all
pupils in the 14-16 age group. Arrangements for the 16-plus
examination should permit candidates to submit landscape models
for assessment as part of their course work.

Aerial or ground level photographs should be compared with
the model. Aerofilms stock oblique aerial photographs of most
of the country and will supply facsimile prints upon request
so that teachers can select those best suited to their
purposes. These will be produced as good quality black-and-
white prints at any specified size, or alternatively as 35mm
slides. The presence of prominent relief features on a high
level oblique aerial photograph will assist its orientation
with map and model provided that allowance is made for the
effect of perspective.

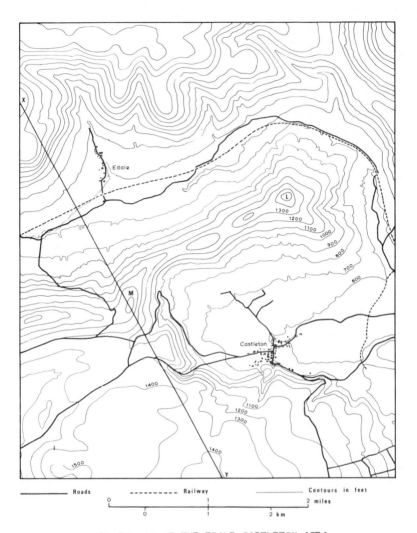

FIGURE 5.1. RELIEF MAP OF THE EDALE—CASTLETON AREA

FIGURE 5.2. DRAINAGE MAP OF THE EDALE-CASTLETON AREA

Ground level photographs taken by the teacher from good
vantage points in the area are a good substitute for, and
frequently better than, photographs taken from the air. Often
the detail is clearer and the precise area to be covered by
each photograph can be determined beforehand. Several photographs of an area taken from different viewpoints may help
pupils to visualise the landscape. The photograph of the Vale
of Edale (Figure 5.3) taken from the slopes of Kinder Scout
near point X on the map (Figure 5.1) looks south-eastwards
across the valley along the line XY and shows all the
distinctive features of relief and land use.

The photograph is used as the basis of an outline sketch.
If a 35 mm slide is projected close to a wall on which is
pinned a sheet of A4 size white paper, the outline of the
landscape can be traced accurately and then transferred to a
spirit master sheet or ink stencil for duplicating purposes.
The slide is projected on to a screen for the pupils to annotate their copies of the sketch. An annotated sketch of
the photograph of the Vale of Edale is shown in Figure 5.4.
Pupils should compare photograph and sketch with map and
model. They should note the effects of perspective and
estimate the distances across the foreground, middleground and
background of the photograph, as well as the distance from the
foreground to the background.

A section can be drawn across the map and where possible
the geology map of the area should be consulted so that the
main rock types can be inserted on the section. A geological
section drawn along the line XY on the map (Figure 5.1),
constructed using the 1:25,000 geology map for this area of
special geological interest, is shown in Figure 5.5. The rock
types can also be painted along the sides of the landscape
model so that the pupils again observe the relationship
between geology and relief. More detailed consideration of a
geology map such as that shown in Figure 5.6 requires an understanding of the rock sequence and inspection of rock specimens.
Thus the oldest rock shown on the Edale-Castleton map is the
jointed, permeable Carboniferous Limestone in the south of the
area. The younger, softer, crumbly Edale Shales have been
eroded to form the embayment around Castleton and the Vale of
Edale itself. The more resistant Mam Tor Sandstone and Shale
Grit form the narrow ridge running from Lose Hill (L on Figure
5.1) to Mam Tor (M). The Grindslow Shales and coarse Kinder-
scout Grit outcrop on the steep slopes to the north of the
Vale of Edale.

Successful map reading and interpretation depends upon a
systematic and methodical approach to the analysis of the
various features of the physical and human landscapes. This
is best provided by a series of questions in the form of a

checklist which the pupils can apply to the map being studied. Thus a checklist for describing a river valley should include the following: trend, width, depth, steepness of sides, and width and gradient of valley floor. If this checklist is applied to the map of the Vale of Edale, the trend is described as being from west to east, or more accurately from west-south-west to east-north-east. The width of the valley, measured between the upper levels of the sides, is about 2 kilometres. The depth of the valley, being the difference in height between the floor and upper levels of the sides, is about 1000 feet. The slopes may be described, in relative terms, as gentle in the lower levels up to 900-1000 feet, and then steepening above 1000 feet. The width of the valley floor is less than one kilometre, and the gradient, as indicated by the spacing of the contours, is gentle.

A checklist for describing a river, as distinct from its valley, should include the direction of flow, the speed of flow, the width, nature of the course, number and size of tributaries, and any man-made alterations. Thus the River Noe is flowing from west to east down the Vale of Edale and its speed, as indicated by the gradient of the valley floor, is probably fairly slow. The River Noe has a winding course and receives many small tributaries on both banks. The width can only be measured if a river is wide enough to be shown by means of a double line. The two ponds may be man-made features. It should be remembered that much precise information about a river can only be verified in the field or from photographs.

Similar checklists for describing upland and lowland areas provide a methodical and systematic way of analysing larger areas of landscape than individual valleys. Thus a checklist for describing an upland area should include trend, landforms, height, types of slopes, steepness of slopes and the lower and upper limits of slopes. Applying this to the area of highland to the south of the Vale of Edale, the landform trends from south-west to north-east and is a ridge, the general height of which is between 1300 and 1500 feet. The lower slopes below 900 feet are gentle and concave, and the upper slopes are steep and convex. The lower slopes rise from the valley floor at about 700 feet and the upper limits are represented by the summits of Mam Tor and Lose Hill, both of which reach a height above 1500 feet.

A checklist for a lowland area may be shorter, indicating trend, landform, general height, and nature of the surface. Thus the lowland area to the south of the ridge is the upper end of a wide vale trending from west to east. It lies at a general height of between 600 and 700 feet and the surface is gently undulating.

FIGURE 5.3. PHOTOGRAPH ACROSS THE VALE OF EDALE

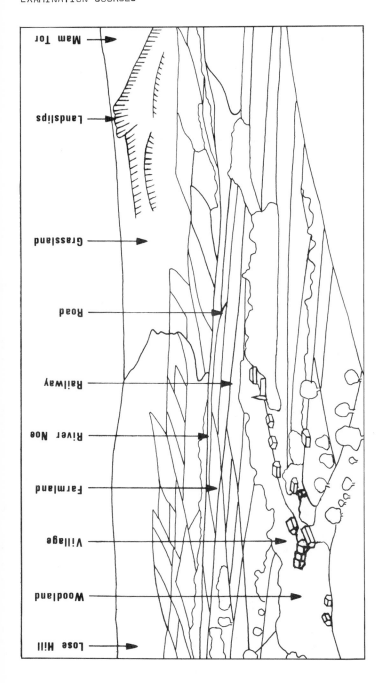

FIGURE 5.4. SKETCH DRAWN FROM PHOTOGRAPH

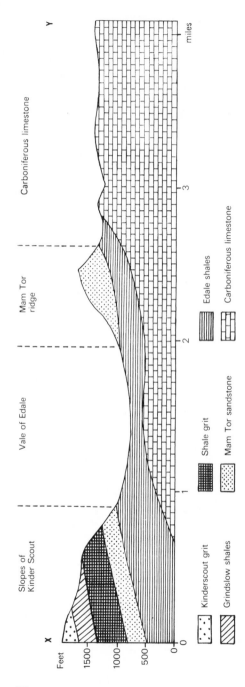

FIGURE 5.5. GEOLOGICAL CROSS SECTION

96

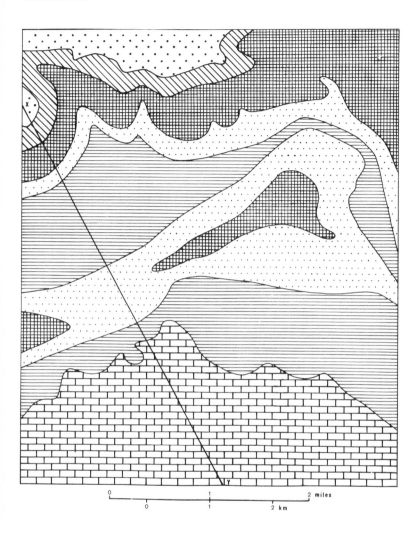

FIGURE 5.6. GEOLOGY MAP OF THE EDALE-CASTLETON AREA
For key see Figure 5.5

The testing of hypotheses or solving of problems is a means of ensuring that the pupil understands the practical applications of map interpretation. Take the statement that 'there is some correspondence between geology and relief'. Reference to the map (Figure 5.1), photograph (Figures 5.3) and cross section (Figure 5.5) should enable the pupil to see that the various sandstones of the Millstone Grit series give rise to the steep, craggy slopes and high plateau of Kinder Scout, reaching an altitude approaching 2000 feet, and to the narrow Mam Tor — Lose Hill ridge on the southern side of the Vale of Edale. The Vale itself, between 600 and 800 feet in height, is cut into the softer, less resistant, crumbly Shales. To the south of Castleton the land then rises by means of slopes which are concave in their lower levels and convex in their upper levels. Again the land rises to a gently undulating plateau, but this time at the lower altitude of 1400 to 1500 feet, on an upstanding mass of jointed Carboniferous Limestone.

As a further example take the statement that 'different drainage patterns develop on different types of geology'. Comparison between the drainage map (Figure 5.2) and cross section (Figure 5.5) shows that a series of north—south flowing streams, fed by small tributaries, have cut deeply incised valleys into the steep Millstone Grit slopes of Kinder Scout. Other streams flow from south to north off the Sandstone slopes of the Mam Tor — Lose Hill ridge. All of these streams are in turn tributaries of the west—east flowing River Noe, cut into the Edale Shales, and together they form a dendritic drainage pattern. This river subsequently turns sharply southwards to join another west—east flowing river in the Edale Shales south of the Mam Tor — Lose Hill ridge, thus forming a kind of trellised drainage pattern. There is a general absence of surface drainage on the permeable, jointed Carboniferous Limestone to the south, but a dendritic pattern of deep, narrow, steep-sided, dry valleys has developed on the slopes of the plateau. At the foot of these slopes the underground drainage emerges as springs near the junction with the Shales.

To ask pupils to search for evidence to support the statement that 'there is some correspondence between geology and relief' or that 'different drainage patterns develop on different types of geology' is to ask them to test hypotheses. Their attention is drawn to a particular matter for investigation more precisely than it is when they are asked to 'describe the relief and drainage'. Pupils who have reached the stage of formal operational thought should be able to reason deductively from the evidence provided by a map.

Aspects of human geography shown on a map should be studied in relation to the physical environment. Lines of communication in particular are often strongly influenced by relief. The road and railway which follow the floor of the Vale of Edale appear as prominent features on the map (Figure 5.1) only because of the thickness of the lines used to represent them. They are relatively insignificant features on the photograph (Figure 5.3). The winding route of the narrow road can be compared with that of the direct route of the railway and related to gradient. At its point of entry on the eastern edge of the map the railway is at an altitude of 600 feet, and at its point of exit from the western edge of the map has risen to an altitude of 800 feet. This rise of 200 feet in a distance of $4\frac{1}{2}$ miles or about 25,000 feet represents a gradient of 1 in 125 or 0.8%.

As evidence to support the statement that 'relief exerts a control over transport routes' the gentle gradient of a railway line following a valley floor can be compared with the steeper gradient of a road at the head of a valley. The main road to the west of Castleton ascends from an altitude of 700 feet to one of 1300 feet by means of the hairpin bend below Mam Tor. This is an ascent of 600 feet in $1\frac{1}{2}$ miles or about 8,000 feet, representing a gradient of 1 in 13 or 7.5%. The more direct route followed by the minor road up the narrow Winnats Pass has an even steeper gradient, climbing 600 feet in 1 mile or 5280 feet and giving a gradient of 1 in 9 or 11%.

The statement that 'geology exerts a control over transport routes' can be used as the basis of a problem solving exercise. The hairpin bend on the road below Mam Tor has been subject to persistent subsidence as a result of its location on the soft shales underlying the sandstone. The widening cracks are now beyond repair and the road is permanently closed to all traffic. The problem is to plan a new route for this road, given that Winnats Pass is too narrow and steep to carry heavy traffic. Its solution demands detailed study of the Ordnance Survey map and requires consideration of the additional need for a by-pass to avoid the narrow main street of Castleton. The route eventually chosen by the highway authorities climbs up Pin Dale on to the limestone plateau south of Castleton.

The kind of work illustrated in this section using maps, model, photographs and cross section, and involving landscape description followed by hypothesis testing and problem solving, should ideally be undertaken in conjunction with the first-hand study of the area in the field. Field courses for pupils in the fourth or fifth form of the secondary school should always be preceded by a thorough study of the area in

the classroom using the procedures described. An example of
a field course based on a problem solving exercise in the
Edale-Castleton area is included in Chapter 7.

GYSL and Avery Hill

The Geography for the Young School Leaver (GYSL) project has
had an important effect on courses for 14-16 year-old pupils.
The Schools Council initially funded the GYSL project at Avery
Hill in 1970 for three years but subsequently agreed to support
it until 1985. Successive extensions have been granted mainly
for dissemination and co-ordination, the detailed strategy for
which has been discussed by Boardman (1980). GYSL materials
have been purchased by more than 2,000 schools in England and
Wales, about 40 per cent of the comprehensive secondary schools
in these two countries. About 100 schools in Scotland and
Northern Ireland have also obtained them. In terms of national
impact the project has been described as 'the jewel in the
Council crown' (MacDonald and Walker, 1976).

The aim of GYSL was to examine the contribution that
geography could make to the education of pupils of average to
below average ability between the ages of 14 and 16, and to
produce schemes of work and supporting resources that could be
used either in a subject or in an interdisciplinary framework.
The project team produced three theme-based kits of materials
which consist of pupils' resource sheets, filmstrips, overhead
transparencies and audiotapes (Schools Council, 1974, 1975).

A teacher's guide accompanies each of the three themes.
This contains comprehensive notes of guidance for the teacher.
There is an emphasis on changes in geography as a discipline
in recent years, especially the move from descriptions of
individual and unique phenomena to a search for recurring
processes and patterns. This requires the investigation of
basic spatial concepts such as location, distance, accessibility
and areal association as well as a consideration of spatial
problems of an economic, environmental, political and social
nature.

An objectives-based model of curriculum design is employed
with a cyclical process involving the formulation of objectives,
choice of learning experiences and use of evaluation techniques.
Objectives are grouped into three broad categories: ideas,
skills, and values and attitudes. The key ideas are usually
derived from important concepts, such as that of accessibility,
whilst case studies contain the specific facts which help the
pupil to understand the ideas. Pupils use a wide range of
skills in working through the themes, such as interpreting
data, analysing statements and communicating through writing,
drawing and discussion. The development of values and

attitudes is fostered through a consideration of social and
environmental issues upon which there are often differing
viewpoints.

The project materials form the basis of a two year course.
Some exercises are given in detail but rigidity of approach is
avoided. The intention is to give guidance to teachers whilst
leaving them free to adapt and use the resources in the ways
they consider most appropriate for their classes. The styles
of learning advocated are pupil centred. The pupils may at
different times be working individually, in groups, or as a
class. Whatever the organisation pupils should be actively
involved in learning through examining evidence, interpreting
data, or discussing values and attitudes held by different
people. This may be contrasted with the heavy emphasis upon
note making and learning factual material in traditional CSE
and O-level courses.

GYSL materials make a contribution towards the development
of graphicacy in pupils through the maps and aerial photographs
included in some of the units. Only limited use is made of
Ordnance Survey maps, however, and they are introduced at
various points in the project materials. Without systematic
training in the basic skills of map reading and interpretation
pupils who are below average in ability would probably have
difficulty with some of the extracts. There are nevertheless
some good instances of the close juxtaposition of large scale
maps with aerial photographs of urban areas.

It has always been the intention of the project that
national curriculum development should be supplemented by
local materials produced by groups based on LEAs. One of the
functions of these groups is to collect local resources, such
as maps and aerial photographs, and develop them into local
units. In an example of the development of a local curriculum
unit Boardman (1976b) uses a low level oblique aerial photograph in conjunction with a 1:2,500 scale map of a small
suburban area and a line drawing indicating the positions of
important features. A second aerial photograph, taken from a
higher altitude and covering a larger area, is used in conjunction with a 1:10,000 map and line drawing. Subsequent
work in the unit involves the use of smaller scale maps,
including a topological map derived from a 1:25,000 map, and a
number of exercises based on 1:50,000 and 1:100,000 maps.
Other examples of locally produced materials are contained in
a collection illustrating ways in which GYSL project ideas and
materials have been adapted for use with disadvantaged pupils
(Boardman 1981d).

All 13 CSE examination boards operate schemes based on GYSL. Most of these are Mode 3, in which teachers devise the syllabus and are responsible for internal assessment, subject to external moderation. Assessment generally consists of a combination of final examination paper and continuously assessed coursework. Because of the very large number of CSE syllabuses based on GYSL which have been submitted, 10 examinations boards are now operating Mode 2 schemes, in which teachers devise the syllabus but give responsibility for assessment to the board. This enables the board to carry out the assessment procedures more economically and reduces the workload on teachers. One CSE board has initiated a Mode 1 scheme based on GYSL, thus assuming responsibility for both syllabus and examination.

The large number of examination papers that are being produced annually makes it difficult to assess the extent to which they test map skills. Nevertheless the universal inclusion of data in the form of maps, diagrams and graphs in these papers means that pupils are constantly having to show their ability to deal with spatially presented data. The cost of Ordnance Survey map extracts and aerial photographs may explain their restricted use in CSE Mode 3 examination papers.

Many of the GYSL ideas and resources are as appropriate for use with the more able pupils as with those of more modest ability. As a result an O-level syllabus and scheme of assessment is now administered jointly by the Welsh Board and Southern Universities Joint Board on behalf of all GCE examinations boards. The O-level scheme, designated Avery Hill to distinguish it from GYSL, is based on the three themes published by the project and a fourth devised by teachers in a school or group of schools. The content of this fourth theme, called a further curriculum unit, must be in physical, regional or applied geography, to complement those on urban, economic, and recreational geography in the published themes. 40 per cent of the total marks are awarded for work done in the further curriculum unit and for course studies completed by the pupils. Both the further curriculum unit and the course studies are internally assessed by teachers in consultation with regional moderators. The examination paper on the three published themes accounts for the other 60 per cent of the total marks.

The style of examining in the Avery Hill O-level paper reflects the kinds of teaching and learning promoted by the project. Questions are truly data response in type, incorporating maps, diagrams, photographs, graphs, tables and other material. An Ordnance Survey map extract is usually included but the question is not compulsory, as it is in conventional O-level examinations. Furthermore, the kinds of question set on Ordnance Survey maps tend to be more imaginative and less stereotyped than in conventional papers. Thus candidates may be asked to name the kinds of leisure activities which are likely to be undertaken at specific locations, and suggest possible reasons for the amount and type of open space in different residential areas. They may then have to decide on the factors which would have to be taken into account before planning permission is granted for building a sports centre on a specified site.

The extension of GYSL to cover the full ability range has enabled teachers to adopt a common core curriculum in geography for all their fourth and fifth form pupils. Schools no longer have to divide pupils into O-level and CSE groups at the beginning of their courses. The project has in effect shown that it is possible for pupils to follow a common course which leads to examinations at different levels at 16-plus.

Geography 14-18

The Geography 14-18 Project, established at Bristol in the same year as GYSL, was initially funded by the Schools Council for four years (1970-1974) and was granted a one-year extension for dissemination. After a gap of three years, funds were provided for further dissemination from Leeds (1978-1980). The project has initiated a programme of curriculum development for more able pupils which is designed to provide them with an intellectually exacting study of geography. Despite its title, the project, because of limited resources and the time needed to make changes in the O-level examination system, actually dealt only with the 14-16 age range.

The project has shown that there can be little change in geography teaching for the 14-16 age group until the examination itself is changed. The form of the examination at O-level determines much of the work done in the classroom. The board's examiners devise questions to permit the ranking of candidates; teachers work towards the most predictable questions; and pupils achieve results in terms of examination passes. All this involves a heavy dependence upon note making, factual learning and reproduction of memorised material in the examination room.

In an attempt to overcome this problem the project has devised a new O-level examination system which fosters school-based curriculum development. This O-level scheme is a considerable innovation in that only 50% of the final marks are allocated for performance in an examination paper set by the Cambridge Board, which operates the scheme on behalf of all

EXAMINATION COURSES

GCE examinations boards. This paper examines a core syllabus
including both human and physical geography, but with a
weighting towards the former. The remaining 50% of the marks
are awarded for two types of internally assessed and externally
moderated coursework: five assessment units devised by teachers,
each representing about two weeks study (30%) and an individual
study carried out by each pupil, usually based on fieldwork
(20%). In this way teachers become more fully involved in the
process of school-based curriculum development.

    Geography 14-18 has published a handbook for school-based
curriculum development (Tolley and Reynolds, 1977) which
provides a comprehensive guide to the project's O-level scheme.
In addition five sets of exemplar materials have been assembled
by groups of teachers with the assistance of the project team.
Each consists of teacher's notes and pupils' resource sheets,
either as class sets or in the form of reproducible master
sheets (Schools Council, 1978, 1980).

    The syllabus for the Geography 14-18 project is itself an
innovation, running to 33 pages and covering a core syllabus,
coursework and individual studies. The aim of the core
syllabus is 'to enable pupils to use important skills, ideas
and models drawn on in geography to classify and interpret
such everyday experiences as discerning order in landscape
and bringing regional and world problems into appropriate
frames of reference'. To achieve this aim, schools or local
consortia are encouraged to plan their own curricula, using
illustrative examples drawn from both the physical and human
branches of geography.

    The syllabus states specifically that one or more of the
twelve questions in the final examination paper will involve
the use of either a 1:25,000 or 1:50,000 map. As in the
GYSL O-level examination paper, the Ordnance Survey map
question is optional, and the questions set are designed to
encourage candidates to search for specific kinds of evidence
provided by the map extract. Thus, instead of a conventional
question asking candidates to describe the relief and drainage
of an area, they are more likely to be asked to quote map
evidence that there is some correspondence between the drainage patterns and the relief of the area.

    Coursework units are studies developed from the core
syllabus which cannot be adequately assessed under time-limit
conditions, for example, because they entail persistence and
initiative on the part of the pupil, or where studies are
specific to a school's local area or a teacher's special
interest and expertise. Studies are selected from five
categories, including those based on regions, the physical
environment or planning problems. The difference between

coursework and other work is one of emphasis and depth of
treatment. The examples given in the project's handbook show
that they encourage the pupils' capacities to explore and
evaluate ideas, to develop problem-solving strategies and to
form and justify practical judgements. There are thus opportunities for the use of Ordnance Survey maps on different
scales in the classroom and in the field. Indeed, coursework
plays an important part in preparing pupils for individual
studies because of the emphasis on study in depth and the use
of local resources. ·Coursework is intended to foster the
pupils' capacity to work individually and to develop their
enquiry skills in undertaking fieldwork.

Individual studies enable pupils to pursue in depth
aspects of geography which are of special interest to them.
They provide experience of self-directed enquiry which introduces them to the demands which the subject makes at sixth form
level. Pupils have to identify a problem, define the objectives of the study, and decide what evidence is needed and how
to collect it. Subsequently pupils have to collect and record
the evidence, analyse and interpret it, and reach conclusions
in relation to the original objectives of the investigation.
Examples of individual studies are: Is meander width proportional to meander length along a river? Is the discharge of
streams related to the area of their drainage basins? Can
separate areas devoted to particular kinds of shops be delimited in the central area of a town? In what ways do the
types of factories outside a town's ring road differ from
those inside it? Individual studies are expected to be about
2,000 words in length and illustrated with maps, diagrams or
photographs.

The contrasting strategies of the Geography 14-18 and
GYSL projects will be apparent. The order of priorities in
GYSL dissemination strategy was first, materials production;
second, teacher involvement; third, examination renewal.
Geography 14-18 reversed these priorities, putting examination
renewal first, since this then facilitated full teacher
involvement, which in turn resulted in the preparation of
teaching materials. Ideas from the Geography 14-18 O-level
scheme have spread downwards to pupils of average ability as
teachers negotiated parallel CSE courses. Conversely, GYSL
ideas have spread upwards to pupils of above average ability
after the successful negotiation of its own O-level scheme.
The two projects which travelled along apparently different
paths eventually arrived at a similar destination. At the
same time they demonstrated the feasibility of a common system
of examining at 16-plus.

EXAMINATION COURSES

The Cambridge Board and East Midlands Board are now jointly providing a GCE/CSE examination in geography based on the Schools Council Geography 14-18 Project. Candidates take either paper 1, which is the same as the Geography 14-18 O-level paper, or paper 2, in which the questions are more highly structured but based on the same resources, including Ordnance Survey map. Thus in paper 1 candidates may be asked to discuss evidence on the map which supports or contradicts generalisations such as 'relief is a major control on transport routes' or 'settlement is usually associated with nodal points in the transport network'. In paper 2 the attention of candidates is drawn to the winding route of a motorway under construction. They are asked to examine five bends in turn and in each case suggest why the planners chose that particular route. The examination paper accounts for 60% of the total marks, the remaining 40% being awarded for school based assessment which is common to all candidates. This weighting represents a slight shift from the 50%-50% balance of the Geography 14-18 O-level but is in line with the Avery Hill 60%-40% weighting.

A single system of examining at 16-plus ends the duplication of work caused by the dual O-level and CSE system. Much time and energy are expended in operating one examination system for pupils in the top 20 per cent of the ability range and another for those in the next 40 per cent of the range. Teachers have the difficult task of deciding which pupils should be entered for each examination and, if the syllabuses are different, decisions have to be taken on pupils at the age of 14. There remains the unresolved problem of providing courses for the 40 per cent of pupils for whom neither O-level nor CSE are designed.

The recommendation that there should be a single system of examining at 16-plus was first made by the Schools Council in 1970. The feasibility of a common system was subsequently investigated by means of experimental joint 16-plus examinations in several subjects, including geography, administered by consortia of GCE and CSE boards. The evidence provided by these experimental examinations again enabled the Schools Council in 1976 to recommend a common system to the Secretary of State, who responded by setting up a steering committee under the chairmanship of Sir James Waddell to make 'an intensive and systematic study of the outstanding problems'. The Waddell report was published in 1978, accepted that a common system was desirable and concluded that it was educationally feasible. In 1980 the then Secretary of State authorised preparatory work to be undertaken on a new examining system but by 1982 his successor was still unable to give a starting date for the new system.

6 Advanced Studies

Every year geography is taken at the Advanced Level of the
General Certificate of Education by nearly 40,000 candidates,
making it the fifth largest subject in terms of entries. All
of the eight GCE examinations boards have revised their A-
level geography syllabuses in recent years. Most sixth form
students are introduced to geological, soil and land utilisation maps. Statistical analysis is now an integral part of
A-level work and the application of statistical techniques to
the analysis of maps is illustrated in this chapter. Subsequently consideration is given to the role of field research
in the individual studies undertaken by students and submitted
for assessment as part of the A-level examination. The
chapter concludes with an outline of the work of the Schools
Council Geography 16-19 project in developing a new A-level
syllabus which promotes enquiry-based learning within a man-
environment curriculum framework.

A-level

The reformed syllabuses introduced by the examinations boards
place an emphasis upon interrelationships between the physical
and human components of the environment. Theory, based on
well-known models, and quantification, involving statistical
techniques, play prominent parts in the new syllabuses, some
of which also stress systems. Several boards make provision
for the submission of work based on an individual field study
as part of the examination. The papers themselves contain
questions requiring essay answers and data response questions,
in which candidates are presented with maps, diagrams, graphs,
photographs and tables for analysis.

The A-level syllabus of the Joint Matriculation Board
leads students towards an understanding of how and why differences exist between different areas of the earth, and this
involves 'an understanding of the processes affecting the
natural environment, an appreciation of interrelationships

within the environment and an awareness of man's role in
producing changes within it'. The Associated Examining Board
syllabus is 'based on the relationships between man and his
environment, their spatial consequences and the resulting
regional patterns'. The London syllabus aims to enable the
candidate to acquire 'a basic knowledge of the nature and
functioning of physical and human environments, an understanding of their interrelationships and the resulting problems'.
The Oxford and Cambridge Board, however, places even greater
emphasis upon interrelationships: the whole syllabus is based
broadly on a systems approach, in particular with a complex
functioning system centring on the relationship between man
and the land. A system is a combination of elements or components or variables which are held together by linkage
mechanisms. These are observed as processes and a change in
one variable produces effects on the rest of the system.

In addition to studying Ordnance Survey topographical
maps, sixth form students are generally being introduced to at
least three other kinds of maps: those of the Geological
Survey, Soil Survey and Second Land Utilisation Survey.
Geological maps are published for most parts of the country,
although some of the earlier 1:63,360 scale maps are no longer
available and others are gradually being replaced by maps on
the 1:50,000 scale. Geological maps appear as 'solid' editions,
showing the parent rocks, and as 'drift' editions, showing the
superficial deposits; sometimes both solid and drift geology
appear on the same map. The vertical sections at the sides of
the maps, often at a highly exaggerated scale, provide details
of the stratigraphical sequence of rocks. Most maps have
section lines drawn across them and the corresponding cross
sections beneath the maps, sometimes drawn without vertical
exaggeration, illustrate the relationship between geology and
topography. Detailed information about the geology shown on
the maps is contained in handbooks which cover the country by
regions. Soil maps on the 1:63,360 scale are also available
but unfortunately coverage is limited to about one-fifth of
the country.

When beginning a study of geology from maps, sixth form
students will find it easier to start with one of the maps on
the 1:25,000 scale which are available for selected areas of
special geological interest. This larger scale permits the
geology to be delineated in greater detail and contours are
drawn at 25 foot intervals as on 1:25,000 topographical maps.
Some of the larger scale geological maps contain brief com-
mentaries describing the characteristics of the main rocks,
whilst for other sheets there are short books providing more
detail about the geology of these classical areas. Soil maps
have also been produced on the 1:25,000 scale for a few
selected areas but they do not coincide with the areas of

special geological interest.

Wherever possible geology and soil maps should be studied
in conjunction with the corresponding maps of the Second Land
Utilisation Survey, which are published as double sheets on
the 1:25,000 scale. All of the detail on the original topographical map is retained and land use is indicated by means
of colour overprinting. Thus various kinds of arable land
and market gardening are shown in different shades of brown
and lilac respectively, grassland is coloured light green,
woodland dark green, and heath, moorland and rough land yellow,
whilst settlement is shaded grey and industry coloured red.
Each map presents an informative picture of the use of the
land at the time of the survey. Techniques and methods of
interpretation are explained and graded questions and exercises
provided in a series of volumes edited by the Director of the
Survey (Coleman, 1982). These are based on a general land use
model which differentiates between wildscape, farmscape, townscape, marginal fringe and rurban fringe.

Students taking A-level geography courses are expected to
use topographical, geological, soil and land utilisation maps
for a variety of purposes. Those listed by two boards will
suffice as examples. The Joint Matriculation Board specifies
the use of topographical maps for a study and interpretation
of physiography, appreciation of patterns of rural settlements,
understanding of site, situation, layout and morphology of
urban areas, and information concerning transport network
patterns. In addition to geological, soil and land utilisation maps, oblique and vertical air photographs are to be
used as illustration of landscape and for the identification
and interpretation of geographical distributions, such as
landforms, land use, settlements and communications. Practical
work also includes the statistical analysis of data and cartographic presentation.

Similar detail about geographical techniques is provided
by the Oxford and Cambridge Board, mainly in relation to the
collection of information and the cartographic and statistical
treatment of data. The collection of information includes an
understanding of sampling strategies (systematic, random and
stratified) and the reliability of data in relation to the
size of the sample. Primary data sources involve the collection of data in the field and secondary sources include
topographic, thematic and historical maps, parish registers
and other parish documents, rate books and directories, census
reports and enumerators' returns, timetables, newspapers and
local authority and other reports. Cartographic techniques
include the depiction of relief and the presentation of spatial
distributions using isopleths, choropleths, dots and circles.
Statistical analysis includes frequency distributions,

measures of central tendency (mean, median and mode), measures of dispersion, ranking concepts and simple correlation and significance tests.

Only four of the eight boards (AEB, SUJB, Oxford and Cambridge and Welsh) set a compulsory question involving an Ordnance Survey map in the examination. Two boards (JMB and Cambridge) include an Ordnance Survey map question for those candidates who take the practical examination paper, which is an alternative to a fieldwork project; this question is compulsory with Cambridge but optional with JMB. The remaining two boards (London and Oxford) leave the Ordnance Survey map question optional.

The questions set differ from one board to another but two types may be discerned. The first is a conventional essay-type question based on the Ordnance Survey map alone. Thus candidates may be asked to describe and interpret the features of the physical landscape, or to write a description of the major relief features and suggest how they may have been formed. In questions with a human orientation candidates may be asked to comment on the settlement and communication patterns shown on the map, or to compare the pattern of settlement and communications on two different parts of the map. Alternatively they may have to draw annotated sketch maps to indicate the main features of the site, situation and nature of built-up areas such as industrial concentrations.

In the second type of question candidates have to use an Ordnance Survey map extract in conjunction with another sketch map provided, usually either a geological or soil map. They may be asked, using a geological map, to describe the landforms of the area and suggest their possible origins, or, using a soil map, to discuss the relationship between soil associations and the relief and drainage of the area. Sometimes candidates are asked to study specific parts of a map and make a detailed comparison between two or more areas. The comparison of two maps, or of two areas on one map, often involves the use of statistical techniques such as those discussed in the next section.

Map Analysis

Quantification is one of the major changes that have affected A-level work. Students are expected at sixth form level to attempt the statistical analysis of data which leads to increased accuracy and objectivity in describing area based relationships. This may involve calculating, for example, the mean, median, mode and standard deviation. A-level students should also be able to use statistical indices as

ADVANCED STUDIES

descriptions of relationships or association between specific
variables. Examples are correlation coefficients and nearest
neighbour statistics.

Drainage basin morphometry is an aspect of the study of
landforms where increasing emphasis is being given to process
rather than form. Students undertake all of the work from a
published map so that the data is readily available in the
classroom. At the same time when students use the quantitative
approach to the analysis of a drainage basin they become aware
of the limitations of purely descriptive mapwork.

The map of the drainage pattern in the Vale of Edale
(Figure 5.2) is here taken as a worked example. The drainage
basin is delimited by the watershed and the streams are
designated orders. All streams with no tributaries are first
order streams; a second order stream is formed when two first
order streams join; a third order stream is formed when two
second order streams join, and so on. When the number of
streams in each order has been counted the bifurcation ratios
can be calculated. These ratios are those between the number
of streams in one order and the number in the next higher
order, as shown in Table 6.1.

TABLE 6.1. ANALYSIS OF VALE OF EDALE DRAINAGE BASIN

Stream Order	1st	2nd	3rd	4th
Number of Streams	99	20	3	1
Bifurcation Ratios	5:1	7:1	3:1	—
Length of Streams	42km	15km	3km	8km
Average Length	0.42km	0.75km	1km	—

The area of the drainage basin is worked out by placing
a tracing of the basin over squared graph paper and counting
the squares. The lengths of the streams in each order are
measured by means of a piece of cotton thread or a map wheel.
The drainage density is calculated by dividing the total
length of all the streams by the area of the basin. Thus in
the Vale of Edale the area of the drainage basin is $21km^2$,
the total length of all the streams is 68km, and the drainage
density is $3.2km/km^2$.

Students plot graphs to show the relationship between the
number of streams and stream order, and to show the average
length of streams against stream order. Their attention is
then drawn to the limitations of curved line graphs owing to
the difficulty of determining which points lie closest to the

111

line. The data can be transformed into straight line graphs
by plotting the logarithm of the number of streams against
stream order, and the logarithm of the average length of
streams against stream order.

Sixth form students would normally work in pairs or
groups on different drainage basins and them compare results,
for example, on various rock types or at different altitudes.
Nevertheless the procedures are very time consuming as all the
data have to be obtained by measurement from maps. An
electronic calculator can be used to perform the statistical
analysis and a computer program has been prepared by the
Computers in the Curriculum project (Schools Council, 1979).
This will calculate bifurcation ratios, convert lengths of
streams measured in centimetres on the map into total stream
lengths in kilometres, convert drainage basin area measured in
square centimetres on the map into a total basin area in
square kilometres, calculate the drainage density, print the
logarithm of the number of streams and the logarithm of the
average length of streams in each order, and draw graphs of
the number of streams (on a log scale) against stream order
(on an arithmetical scale) and of the average length of
streams (on a log scale) against stream order (on an arithmetical scale). These rapid calculations by the computer
provide results almost immediately, thus eliminating the
drudgery from the calculations and making more time available
for comparisons between different drainage basins.

The extent to which quantitative techniques should be
used in A-level geography courses is a matter of debate. A
clarification has been attempted by Robinson (1981). After
summarising the arguments for and against quantification in
school geography, he concludes that what is important is the
development of an attitude of mind in students so that they
are not afraid of numbers as an important means of description, and accept numerical analysis as one aspect of geographical study. He observes that A-level geography students
should be able to use statistical indices such as correlation
coefficients and nearest neighbour statistics as descriptions
of relationships or association between specific variables.
They should also be able to apply simple statistical tests
such as chi-square.

In a survey of the statistical competence of 375 under-
graduates reading for honours degrees in geography at nine
universities, however, Tidswell (1981) found that only 8 per
cent appreciated the significance of standard error in the
most fundamental data collecting device, sampling. Only 19
per cent understood the use of nearest neighbour analysis as
a means of seeking a measure in a dot distribution and less
than 25 per cent knew when to apply the chi-square test in a

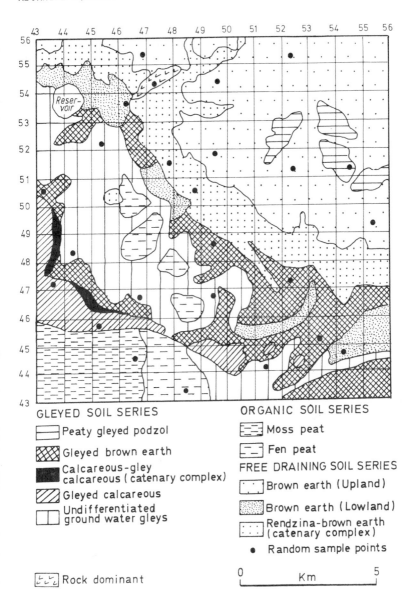

GLEYED SOIL SERIES

☐ Peaty gleyed podzol

▨ Gleyed brown earth

◼ Calcareous-gley calcareous (catenary complex)

▧ Gleyed calcareous

☐ Undifferentiated ground water gleys

☐ Rock dominant

ORGANIC SOIL SERIES

☐ Moss peat

☐ Fen peat

FREE DRAINING SOIL SERIES

☐ Brown earth (Upland)

☐ Brown earth (Lowland)

☐ Rendzina-brown earth (catenary complex)

• Random sample points

0 — Km — 5

FIGURE 6.1. SOIL MAP OF THE WELLS–CHEDDAR AREA

TABLE 6.2. PARENT MATERIALS OF SOIL SERIES IN THE WELLS–CHEDDAR AREA

SOIL GROUP	SOIL SERIES	PARENT MATERIALS
Podzol	Peaty Gleyed Podzol	Non-calcareous Old Red Sandstone
Brown Earth	Free-Draining Brown Earth Upland Series	Loessial Silty Drift of variable depth over Carboniferous Limestone
	Lowland Series	Gravelly Head over Keuper Marl
	Gleyed Brown Earth	Keuper Marl
Gley	Undifferentiated Ground Water Gleys	Riverine & Estuarine Clays
Calcareous	Gleyed Calcareous	Lower Jurassic Calcareous Clay-Shales
Organic	Fen Peat	Slightly Acid to Neutral Peat over Silt-Clays
	Moss Peat	Acid Peat over Silt-Clays
Catenary Complexes	Rendzina-Brown Earth Catena	Carboniferous Limestone & Screes
	Calcareous-Gley Calcareous Catena	Rhaetic Limestone & Clays

given appropriate context. He concludes that whilst many students seem to have acquired a basic facility in using a range of statistical techniques, few know how to interpret the results or appreciate the limitations of the methods used.

The concept of random points is fundamental to many techniques of analysis. A random pattern on a map is one in which the location of each point is not in any way influenced by the location of the remaining points. The pattern is simply produced from two random number tables placed side by side so that the values can be read in pairs. These pairs are then used as the grid co-ordinates for the mapping of a random distribution, the first value providing the easting and the second the northing for the location of a point.

The 25 random sample points shown on the map of the soil series in the Wells-Cheddar area of Somerset (Figure 6.1) have been produced in this way. Those which occur on the gleyed soil series are counted: peaty gleyed podzol (1), gleyed brown earth (4), calcareous-gley calcareous (catenary complex) (0), gleyed calcareous (2), undifferentiated ground water gleys (5). This gives a total of 12 sample points on the gleyed soil series out of the 25 on the map and suggests that 48 per cent of the area may be occupied by the series. The standard error of this estimate is then calculated using the formula

$$SE = \sqrt{\frac{p \times q}{n}}$$

where SE is the standard error

        p is the percentage of occurrences in a specified category

        q is the percentage not in that category

        n is the number of points in the sample

Substituting in the formula

$$SE = \sqrt{\frac{48 \times 52}{25}}$$

$$= \sqrt{\frac{2496}{25}}$$

$$= \sqrt{100}$$

$$= 10$$

The standard error makes it possible to predict with varying degrees of certainty or confidence the accuracy of the estimate of the percentage of the area occupied by the gleyed soil series. Thus there is a 68% probability that the actual percentage of the area occupied by the gleyed soil series lies between + and − 10 from 48, i.e. between 38 and 58 (one standard deviation from the mean on the normal curve of distribution). At the 95% confidence level it can be predicted that the actual percentage lies between + and − 2 × 10 = 20 from 48, i.e. between 28 and 68 (two standard deviations from the mean). At the 99% confidence level it can be predicted that the actual percentage lies between + and − 3 × 10 = 30 from 48, i.e. between 18 and 78 (three standard deviations from the mean).

The table giving information about the parent materials of the major soil groups and soil series (Table 6.2) used in conjunction with the map (Figure 6.1) and an Ordnance Survey 1:50,000 map of the area helps to explain the occurrence of the gleyed soil series in the area. Gleyed soils are those which are periodically waterlogged as a result of poor drainage. Most of the gleyed soils occur in the western and southern parts of the area, much of which consists of a very flat, low lying plain, in places less than 10 metres in altitude. In such circumstances ground water gleys develop because the ground water table in the riverine and estuarine clays approaches the surface, waterlogging much of the soil profile. On the north-eastern side of the plain, where the land rises gently to about 50 metres and the drainage improves, gleyed brown earths have developed on the Keuper Marl on the lower slopes of the Mendip Hills. Similarly, on the south-western side of the plain, the land rises on a ridge of Lower Jurassic calcareous clay shales, on which are found gleyed calcareous soils as well as gleyed brown earths, forming part of a catenary complex with soil profiles associated with relief features. The only gleyed soils found at high altitudes are the peaty gleyed podzols which have developed on the poorly drained Old Red Sandstone at an altitude of about 250 metres, the highest part of the Mendip Hills.

The nucleated settlements in the Wells-Cheddar area are shown in Figure 6.2. How could the pattern be described? Although it is clear that the settlements do not cluster together, is it possible to say whether they are regularly spaced, or is there no apparent order to the pattern? Individual students will give different answers to this question, depending upon their own interpretation of the pattern and their subjective impressions of it. An objective measure is provided by nearest neighbour analysis which makes it possible

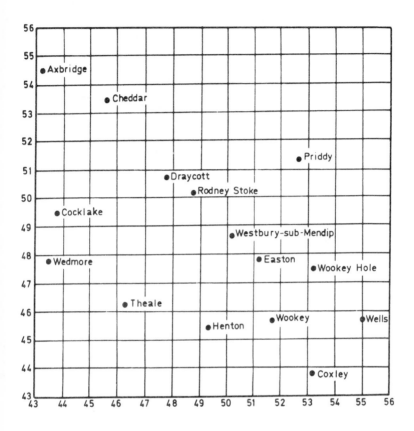

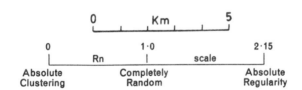

FIGURE 6.2. SETTLEMENT MAP OF THE WELLS—CHEDDAR AREA

TABLE 6.3.   NEAREST NEIGHBOUR MEASUREMENTS IN THE WELLS-CHEDDAR
AREA

SETTLEMENT	NEAREST NEIGHBOUR	DISTANCE (KM)
Axbridge	Cheddar	2.6
Cheddar	Axbridge	2.6
Draycott	Rodney Stoke	1.1
Rodney Stoke	Draycott	1.1
Priddy	Rodney Stoke	4.0
Westbury-sub-Mendip	Easton	1.4
Easton	Westbury-sub-Mendip	1.4
Wookey Hole	Easton	2.0
Wells	Wookey Hole	2.5
Wookey	Wookey Hole	2.4
Coxley	Wookey	2.4
Henton	Wookey	2.4
Theale	Wedmore	3.2
Wedmore	Cocklake	1.8
Cocklake	Wedmore	1.8
	Total	32.7

to predict the average distance that would separate points from their nearest neighbours if the points were located at random throughout the area.

In order to derive the nearest neighbour statistic of the settlement pattern shown on the map the distance from each settlement to its nearest neighbour is measured, as shown in Table 6.2. The total of 32.7 km for fifteen measurements gives a mean of 2.2 km. The nearest neighbour statistic is derived from

$$Rn = 2\bar{d}\sqrt{\frac{n}{A}}$$

where Rn is the nearest neighbour statistic

$\bar{d}$ is the mean distance (km) apart of the points in the pattern

n is the number of points in the pattern

A is the area (sq km) of the map extract

Substituting in the formula

$$Rn = 2\bar{d}\sqrt{\frac{n}{A}}$$

$$Rn = 2 \times 2.2\sqrt{\frac{15}{13 \times 13}}$$

$$= 4.4\sqrt{\frac{15}{169}}$$

$$= 4.4\sqrt{.09}$$

$$= 4.4 \times .3$$

$$= 1.32$$

The scale given below the map (Figure 6.2) indicates that if Rn is less than 1.0 the observed average distance is smaller than the expected value. For this result to be achieved the points would have to be closer together than in a random situation and the pattern would therefore be described as clustered, a completely clustered pattern producing a value of 0. If Rn exceeds 1.0, however, the observed average distance is greater than the expected value. This indicates that the points tend to be more regularly spaced than in a random situation. If all points are spaced with perfect regularity they are arranged like a lattice of equilaterial triangles, each point being equidistant from the other points, and Rn reaches its maximum value of 2.15. The Rn value derived from the analysis of a map can thus be placed on the scale and an appropriate interpretation made. The value also makes possible an objective comparison with the pattern on any other map.

Reference to the Rn scale shows that the value of 1.32 for the Wells-Cheddar area lies nearly one-third the way between a completely random pattern (1.0) and one of absolute regularity (2.15). It is pertinent to ask about the extent to which this statistic reflects the settlement pattern on the map. There is an apparently regular linear pattern of settlements along the foot of the scarp slope of the Mendip Hills from Axbridge to Wells, and another along a low ridge which extends westwards from Wells to Wedmore. The settlement pattern, therefore, is related to altitude and slope, but the nearest neighbour statistic cannot take these into account. Because it is based only on measurement of distance it assumes a uniform surface. Another limitation to the statistic is set by the boundaries of the map. The nearest neighbours of some settlements which are located near the edges of the map, such as Axbridge and Wedmore, may lie just off the map. Furthermore, the north-east quadrant, comprising the Mendip Hills, contains only one settlement (Priddy) and the northern third of the map contains only two (Axbridge and Cheddar). If the northern boundary of the map had been grid line 51 instead of 56 the nearest neighbour statistic might have been higher, indicating a more regular pattern. Statistics need to be evaluated critically, and their limitations should be appreciated.

Field Research

The practical work in which students are involved when analysing data on maps often leads to work in the field which forms part of most A-level geography courses. Individual field studies provide students with their first opportunity to engage in genuine field research. They identify a problem, formulate a hypothesis, collect their own data in the field, analyse and interpret the data, accept or reject the hypothesis, and draw their own conclusions. The sequence of activities is broadly similar to that recommended at O-level by the Geography 14-18 project, except that the field study has to be undertaken in greater depth, measurements are usually required to confirm or refute a hypothesis, statistical tests may be applied, and the resulting report usually runs to about 4,000 words.

The Associated Examining Board is the only one which makes the submission of an individual fieldwork report compulsory for all candidates. It must consist of a single field investigation and show evidence of direct observation in the field. The fieldwork study presents students with the opportunity to investigate a topic of their own choice in some depth, to show initiative in searching for information and to draw conclusions from it. Students are expected to show in their reports the ability to identify and define objectives for field investigation; to collect appropriate data; to process and present the data and interpret the findings; to express information in a clear and concise form; and to evaluate the results and express their findings in the form of conclusions. The assessment of the reports is done by an examiner from outside the school, who requires each student to attend an oral examination lasting about 30 minutes. This oral examination is devoted entirely to the assessment of the fieldwork investigation. It provides the students with an opportunity to discuss their work and to supplement it with additional notes and samples. Up to 20 per cent of the total marks for the examination are awarded for the fieldwork investigation.

Four other boards, Cambridge, Oxford and Cambridge, SUJB and JMB, allow students to submit a report on their fieldwork for assessment as an alternative to taking one of the examination papers. Cambridge pioneered the local geography scheme whereby candidates receive credit for an individual study, up to 23 per cent of the total marks being awarded for it, the same as for the practical paper. Each study takes the form of a written account not exceeding 4,000 words in length and illustrated with relevant maps, diagrams and photographs. The account should provide a clear statement of the problem, the methods of enquiry adopted, and the results and conclusions obtained. Candidates are given interviews on the completed studies by an examiner, who must be able to see their original field notebooks.

The Oxford and Cambridge Board operates a similar scheme although it is called a local geography essay. It must nevertheless be based on the student's own observations and researches, and may be up to 4,000 words in length. The essay gives the student the opportunity to demonstrate the ability to collect and analyse information, and to develop cogent arguments rather than to write descriptively. Assessment includes an oral examination at which students must produce their field notebooks.

The Southern Universities Joint Board permits students to submit a local study up to 4,000 words in length instead of taking a paper devoted to a practical exercise. The study should be based on a clearly defined problem or hypothesis and must be an original piece of work. Teachers assess the work of their students in accordance with specified criteria and may award up to 20 per cent of the total marks for the local study. Samples of work are called in by the board but candidates are not interviewed.

The Joint Matriculation Board is unusual in permitting students to submit either one major practical project or three small scale practical projects. Either of these options may be chosen as an alternative to the practical paper. The projects are intended to test the student's abilities to use the skills and techniques relevant to the syllabus. Projects should be related to clearly defined areas of study and may involve the testing of theoretical ideas in real situations or the application of quantitative techniques. As in the SUJB scheme, teachers assess the work of their students according to specified criteria and up to 20 per cent of the total marks may be awarded for the practical projects. The JMB uses external statistical moderation procedures and candidates are not interviewed.

The remaining three boards encourage fieldwork and may set questions on it in the examination but do not make provision for candidates to submit fieldwork projects. The London Board, for example, regards field and practical work as an integral part of the syllabus. Students should be trained in field observation, data collection and the use of some simple instruments. The Oxford Board expects students to be familiar with elementary fieldwork methods and data collection, presentation and interpretation. The Welsh Board encourages fieldwork undertaken in the local area or elsewhere. Examination questions on fieldwork set by all three of these boards are optional so that candidates could still pass without having carried out fieldwork.

When students begin a piece of field research they should always define carefully the problem they intend to investigate. It is best to frame it in the form of a question so that the objectives of the investigation are clear and precise, and the study itself is of manageable proportions. The study of maps and observations in the field should suggest to the student ideas which could lead to the framing of a specific question. Examples are: To what extent does the form of a particular upland valley correspond to the theoretical form of the valley of a stream in its upper stage? What is the relationship between stream discharge and rainfall in a small catchment area? Sometimes a well known model can provide the framework for a study: How well does the Von Thunen model predict land use around a town? To what extent do the

residential zones of a town correspond to those in the
Burgess model?

Field research on rivers might well develop out of an
initial analysis based on maps. A student investigating the
form of an upland valley could begin by drawing sections across
the valley from the map and then supplementing them with more
accurate and detailed cross sections constructed in the field
with the aid of ranging poles. A similar method would be
used for constructing a longitudinal profile of the valley.
This procedure ensures that the student acquires a spatial
conception of the valley. The sections and profile would also
be supplemented by the field plotting of a morphological or
slope facet map on a large scale base map. This encourages
the student to make a systematic study of the characteristic
features of a valley before selecting those features which
merit a more detailed examination of processes and relationships.

If measurements have to be made it will be necessary to
formulate a hypothesis to direct the line of enquiry. A study
of streams emerging from limestone areas could include the use
of a chemical test to measure the calcium carbonate concentration in the water. The student could either investigate
the spatial variation at different points on one stream, or
alternatively compare two streams in different catchment areas.
In the first investigation the student could test the hypothesis
that the calcium carbonate concentration increases with
distance downstream; in the second investigation the hypothesis
would be that calcium carbonate concentration in one stream
will be greater than that in the other stream. Other studies
of stream channels could test hypotheses about stream flow
characteristics in relation to the sinuosity of meanders and
their pool and riffle features, or the sediment load and its
characteristics at different points downstream. The places
at which measurements are made should be carefully plotted on
a map so that they are placed in a spatial setting.

The collection and recording of data to answer a question
or test a hypothesis should involve a consideration not only
of the type of data and the method by which it can be collected but also of the constraints of sampling. The purpose
of sampling is to save time in data collection whilst
permitting valid conclusions to be reached. In this respect
the discussion in the previous section on random point
sampling in the analysis of maps applies equally to the collection of data at random locations in the field. The standard error of the sample provides a statistical measure of
the confidence with which conclusions about a sample can be
interpolated to a whole population. Statistical tests will
be appropriate to a range of studies, and tests of correlation

to describe the relation between two sets of variables are
particularly useful.

The analysis of data should be supported by maps to show
that spatial patterns have been investigated. Maps may be
accompanied by diagrams, graphs and photographs where appropriate. The analysis and interpretation of the data should be
followed by an attempt to explain the phenomena which have
been investigated before conclusions are reached. The
original hypothesis may be accepted or rejected, possibly
leading to the formulation of new ideas, since research is a
continuous process. The steps described here are the main
stages in geographical field research and correspond to the
procedures of scientific method.

The Geography 16-19 project, the work of which is
described in the next section, has extended and elaborated
upon these stages for students when they undertake their
individual studies. The project takes the view that geographical enquiry encompasses not only the handling and analysis
of 'hard' geographical data but also the analysis and clarification of attitudes and values relevant to the question or
problem under consideration. The project has outlined a route
for enquiry within the man-environment approach to geography.
The route indicates that study usually begins with consideration of a question, problem or issue. This is then investigated by following the stages of description, analysis,
explanation, evaluation and decision making. The procedure
is discussed in detail by Rawling (1981a) in relation to the
investigation of local issues by means of an enquiry based
approach. An example of field enquiry involving a consideration of attitudes and values as well as the analysis of data
about an urban road planning problem is included in Chapter 7.

Geography 16-19

In addition to the two curriculum projects in geography for
the 14-16 age group, the Schools Council has also funded a
third project, Geography 16-19, to promote curriculum development for this older age range. Although the project was
initially funded for four years (1976-80) at the University of
London Institute of Education, the Schools Council subsequently
undertook to support it until 1984. Teachers and lecturers
participating in the project have been involved in a re-
consideration of the objectives, content and teaching methods
of geography courses for the 16-19 age group in schools, sixth
form colleges, and colleges of further education. Through
this involvement teachers in these institutions have been
helped to appreciate the significance of their role as curriculum developers.

The developmental work of Geography 16-19 has been concerned with objectives, content and teaching methods not only for the more able students following GCE Advanced Level courses but also the 'new' sixth formers with lower academic aspirations pursuing one-year courses leading to the pilot Certificate of Extended Education (CEE). For this purpose the project has devised a curriculum framework for geography courses for 16-19 year-old students. This is based on a man-environment approach to geography, in which geographical study is focused on questions, problems and issues arising from the interrelationship of people with their environments. The project believes that this approach to geographical study may be appropriately developed through a process of enquiry, in which students discuss the questions, problems and issues, consider relevant aspects of geographical theory, and arrive at solutions or a range of possible solutions.

The starting point for studying a topic is a question, problem or issue arising from the way people interact with their varied environments. Study proceeds by means of a route for enquiry involving clarification of the question, analysis, evaluation and finally a return to the question or issue in order to attempt to provide a solution or answer. Students handle original sources, plot data and undertake research as well as listening to talks and participating in discussion. They may work in groups, take on roles, simulate a situation, lead a discussion, identify their own value position, and if necessary defend this in writing or verbally. The teacher's role is less that of an information giver and director of activities than that of partner in the enquiry. The teacher may have to guide and direct enquiry but students have ample opportunity to organise their own activities, turning to their teacher for help and advice when necessary. In enquiry-based learning the teacher may participate in discussion or role play alongside the students and his or her opinion is one of several considered.

A man-environment approach to the study of geography is based on the recognition that the interaction of people in and with their varied environments provides certain distinctive spatial locations, distributions and associations, and that various flows or movements of goods, people, ideas and objects take place. Man-environment interactions often give rise to questions which are worth answering, or problems and issues which involve conflict and controversy. Such an issue is posed by the question 'How may conflicting demands for use of land in a densely populated area best be managed?'. In the course of their investigations students are encouraged to ask the key questions asked by geographers and to use the enquiry techniques used by geographers, so that they work towards an understanding of the organising ideas and concepts of the subject. Students thus ask important questions about environmental problems and the quality of life in the modern world, and at the same time develop an understanding of the nature of geography as a discipline and the methods of working used by its practitioners.

Geography 16-19 has identified four man-environment themes around which courses are constructed. These are: Natural environments - the challenge for man; Use and misuse of natural resources; Man-environment issues of global concern; Managing man-made environments and systems. The project has developed a new A-level syllabus which runs to 39 pages and is being administered by the London Board on behalf of all other boards. The A-level course structure is different from all existing ones in that it is composed of a series of modules, each representing about six weeks of teaching time in length. A module is defined as a unit of study which is self-contained in terms of logical development of principles and of learning within it, but has recognisable links with other modules. This modular structure is an extension of an idea developed by a group of teachers in the West Midlands (Boardman, 1978). There are six compulsory core modules in the Geography 16-19 A-level syllabus, including at least one in each of the four man-environment themes. Thereafter teachers have considerable freedom in course structure, selecting three option modules out of a total of 24 listed in the syllabus. Furthermore, a special option module, devised by the teacher, may replace one of the three option modules if desired. Each module poses a set of man-environment questions, problems or issues, and enables the student to investigate them by means of the appropriate branches of geographical enquiry.

The emphasis upon interrelationships in the environment accords with that in other revised A-level syllabuses already noted. Thus in the Geography 16-19 syllabus the candidate is expected to show an understanding of 'the functioning and characteristics of both natural and human systems and their interrelationships', and should be familiar with 'methods of recognising, describing and analysing the spatial consequences of man-environment interrelationships'. Students should master a range of intellectual, social, communication, practical and study skills 'including particularly the ability to use and prepare maps of different types and scales.' Techniques of map interpretation should be based not only on topographical maps at 1:25,000 and 1:50,000 scales but also those at 1:10,000 scales and larger, together with the 1:25,000 land utilisation maps. Teachers are encouraged to include mapwork wherever appropriate in the syllabus, although there is no module where mapwork is specifically required.

The assessment structure for A-level has been specially designed for the course. The core modules are assessed by means of two external examination papers (55% of the total marks) and the option modules are assessed by coursework set and marked by the teacher (30%). Each student also has to complete an individual study based on an original piece of field enquiry, which is marked by the board (15%). The first of the two papers is an innovation in that it consists of a decision making exercise designed to assess the student's ability to undertake geographical enquiry. Candidates are faced with a particular environmental question, problem or issue to consider, in the form of a case study, and are provided with information and data concerning the issue. They have to examine the evidence and reach a decision about the issue. The specimen examination paper consisting of a decision-making exercise concerning the location of new shopping development in Abingdon has been reproduced elsewhere (Rawling, 1981b). The second of the two examination papers consists of a series of data response questions on the core modules. Each option module is assessed by means of an essay and a piece of coursework concerned with the application of a technique or techniques to a particular question, problem or issue. The assessment of the individual study based on field enquiry is undertaken by the board and includes an interview with each candidate.

Most of the curriculum development for Geography 16-19 has been undertaken by teachers meeting in local curriculum groups. Teachers have been involved in discussions at meetings, the preparation of materials, trialling in the classroom and evaluation of the results. Since the Certificate of Extended Education (CEE), like the CSE, is administered regionally and not nationally, local groups of teachers have had to devise and submit their own Mode 3 schemes to their regional examinations boards.

The similarities between the Geography 16-19 and Geography 14-18 projects will be apparent. In both cases there has been an emphasis on changing the examination system, involving teachers in school-based curriculum development, and giving teachers some of the responsibility for assessment. The two projects have also encouraged the development of parallel CSE and CEE schemes for pupils of more modest ability. The A-level and CEE courses designed within the Geography 16-19 curriculum framework are natural sequels to the O-level and CSE courses developed within the Geography 14-18 project framework.

7 Fieldwork and Graphicacy

Fieldwork makes an essential contribution to the development of graphicacy in pupils of all ages. The use of the local environment in developing map reading skills in younger pupils was recommended at several points in Chapters 3 and 4, and the role of individual studies in fieldwork in geography courses for older pupils was considered in Chapters 5 and 6. Fieldwork is discussed in more detail in this chapter, essentially by means of four case studies of work with pupils of different ages. Although the first two were carried out with children aged 10-11 in their last year at primary school, they provide examples of the kind of work which might be attempted by children in their first year at secondary school and certainly in the corresponding years of a middle school. The third study illustrates the kind of problem-orientated field course which can be organised for O-level and CSE pupils as part of their examination work. The fourth study is more appropriate for sixth form students because it involves an understanding of local government planning and decision making procedures. It is hoped that these four studies of fieldwork — two urban and local, two rural and residential — will provide an indication of the progression in work with pupils of different ages to which attention is increasingly being directed (Bennetts, 1981; Boardman, 1981a, c; Graves, 1979; Mills, 1981).

A Housing Estate

Modern primary schools place a considerable emphasis on child-centred learning, on the organisation of small group assignments in which children learn from one another, and on the provision of a wide range of resources for learning. Teachers in primary schools are normally class teachers responsible for most of the work of their classes each day. English and mathematics are usually taught as distinct subjects so that basic skills are taught and developed. Other subjects, however, are frequently combined into an interdisciplinary or integrated

framework. Geography, history and biology are often included
in an environmental studies curriculum, which involves a study
of the links between phenomena in the environment and the
whole of which they are a part. The amount of time allocated
to environmental studies is commonly one or two hours per week,
but in some schools it may be one or two half-days or longer.
Occasionally more extended periods are devoted to environmental
work, permitting total integration of the curriculum.

The work described in this section was undertaken by a
class of 35 children of mixed ability aged 10-11 years at
Chivenor Primary School, Birmingham. This school is committed
to educating children about the environment, through the
environment (using the environment as resource material) and
for the environment (developing children's attitudes towards
it). Environmental education is used not only as a means of
teaching and developing basic skills of literacy, numeracy,
oracy and graphicacy, but also as a means of teaching and
practising applied techniques and scientific method. This
approach has been found to produce children who are highly
motivated, show a positive attitude to learning, maintain
interest in their work, and display enthusiasm in investigating
problems which they are capable of understanding and which are
relevant to the modern world. The success of the approach
depends to a large extent on the commitment of the teacher to
the aims of environmental education and belief in the
effectiveness of an integrated curriculum. Tests administered
to children in this particular school, however, suggest that
an integrated curriculum and child-centred teaching methods
improve the children's creative thinking as well as their
academic achievement in reading, number and verbal reasoning
(Palmer, 1981).

The school is situated on the Castle Vale housing estate
which occupies the site of a former airfield on the north-
eastern edge of Birmingham. This is an area of completely
flat land, lacking in landscape features, windswept and poorly
drained. The site measures only one and a half miles square
but was designed to accommodate 25,000 people in dwelling
units consisting of 11 - and 16 - storey high rise flats,
together with maisonettes and town houses. The first people
who moved into Castle Vale in 1965 were tenants selected from
various parts of Birmingham who needed better accommodation.
Subsequently the city's policy of rehousing people from the
inner ring has brought many social and economic problems to
the estate. Families have been faced with higher rents and
heating bills than previously, which made it necessary for
mothers of young families to go to work. Many of the original
families have now left the estate, having been able to buy
their own homes elsewhere. They have been replaced by families

with limited means who are often supported by the Social Services. The population of Castle Vale has now declined to 15,000 and so the estate suffers not only from the bleakness of its environment but also from the emptiness of a third of its dwellings. It should be noted, therefore, that the work outlined below was carried out by children in an adverse setting, but one which is found around many urban schools.

The children undertook the study of their housing estate during their last two terms at the school. Their work was entered for the national 'Wide Awake Trail' competition organised by the Daily Mirror and the Heritage Education Group of the Civic Trust. The entry, under the title 'The Good, the Bad and the Ugly' was awarded first prize in the 1981 competition. It consisted of over 600 pages of children's writing, poetry, drawings, paintings, graphs, maps, plans and photographs, together with a separate folder of large scale maps and an audiotape of interviews with people and songs by the children. Accordingly it is impossible in a brief description to convey the full scope and capture the vitality of the children's work, but further details are available elsewhere (Palmer and Wise, 1982).

At the start of the study the Castle Vale estate had to be established as a distinct unit in the children's minds. They drew a location map of the north-east part of Birmingham and the main lines of communication from the city centre to the estate. They then drew a smaller scale map of Birmingham to show the complete city boundary and the M5 and M6 motorways. This helped the children to appreciate the need for maps on different scales. Having identified Castle Vale as a unit within the city, the children took a preliminary walk around the estate and compiled a list of its main features – houses, shops, services and roads. The first question was asked: had the estate always existed in its present form?

By visiting the Local Studies Department of the Birmingham Central Library the children made tracings of maps of the Castle Bromwich area dated 1802, 1848, 1887 and 1937. These showed that throughout the nineteenth century and early part of the twentieth century most of the area was farmland. The children confirmed this by consulting Kelly's Directories of 1890 and 1903 which listed most of the inhabitants as farmers. During the 1930s part of the area was converted into an air-field for testing spitfires which were built in an adjacent factory. The airfield was extensively used during the second world war and in the postwar years became the civilian Castle Bromwich airfield, eventually closing when nearby Elmdon expanded to become Birmingham Airport.

The development of Castle Vale as a housing estate was investigated by means of a study of the school's admission register. The children went through the register from the date of the school's opening in 1965, and noted the date on which each road was first recorded as being the address of a child. The names of the roads were classified in chronological order of appearance at six-monthly intervals for 1965, 1966, and 1967, and thereafter annually for 1968, 1969 and 1970, when most building on the estate was complete. Using a Geographia road map of the estate as a base, the children compiled four overlays to show, by means of differently coloured rows of buildings, the growth of the estate between 1965 and 1981. They thus collected their data from original documents and converted it into map form.

The children next carried out a study of Castle Vale as it is today. They drew a plan of their school on a scale of 1:100, having previously drawn plans of their classroom and rooms in their homes. They then used the 1:1,250 (50 inches to one mile) Ordnance Survey map of the estate and, orientating their maps with the aid of compasses, they plotted in the field the different types of buildings and other kinds of land use: high rise flats, maisonettes, houses, shops, garages, gardens and open spaces. The results were subsequently trans- ferred in the classroom to the full base map of the estate using a different colour for each category. This work included field sketches of selected buildings which some children also photographed. These included the church, library, residents' club, shops, schools and swimming baths.

Another substantial part of the children's study con- sisted of an investigation of the inhabitants' perceptions of life on the estate. Each of the 35 children wrote down, with reasons, the three features of the estate that he or she thought were the best, the three features considered to be the worst, and the three that were the ugliest. The 105 features in each category were then placed in rank order and bar graphs were drawn to illustrate the results numerically; the best three were the swimming baths, the sports area and the gardens with flowers and trees; the worst three were vandalism, litter throwing and children's behaviour; the ugliest three were litter, graffiti and vandalised houses. The children then asked their parents the same questions and the 105 features were analysed in the same manner, but the results were different. Parents ranked the shopping centre, health centre and swimming baths as the best features; vand- alism, lack of facilities for children and housing as the worst; litter, vandalism and graffiti as the ugliest. Child- ren thus learnt to appreciate differences between their own perceptions and those of their parents. They investigated the different features in each category, sketching, photographing and writing about such good features as trees and flowers, and did some quadrat sampling in the school quadrangle to quantify the different species of urban wildlife growing there. Descriptions of the bad features included the flat nature of the land, the poorly drained, muddy ground, the high density of the housing and the design of individual dwelling units.

The unanimous agreement of children and parents that litter formed the ugliest aspect of the estate led the children to collect litter in the school grounds for a week. They sorted and categorised their collection of 12,224 pieces of litter (much of it blown into the school grounds!) into paper, plastic, polythene, glass and metal. The children then constructed pie charts to show the percentages in each category. They also worked out the area of the school grounds from the plan they had drawn and calculated the number of pieces collected per square metre.

To conclude their study, the children wrote about what life might be like on the estate in twenty years' time. In their recommendation they said what alterations they would have made if they had been involved in planning the estate, and what changes they thought could reasonably be made today. The children concluded that people were both the best and the worst features of life on the estate. Some people planted flowers and trees and cared for the neighbourhood, whilst others caused vandalism and wrote graffiti. Only people could change the estate, and it was the children's responsibility, as the adults of tomorrow, to improve the urban environment for the future enjoyment of all.

The children were taught many basic graphical skills, therefore, during this investigation undertaken as part of an integrated environmental studies curriculum. They learnt to make large scale plans, to draw maps on different scales, to orientate maps out of doors and to plot additional information on them. Furthermore, by comparing a series of historical maps, by converting data from an admission register into map form, and by conducting interviews to obtain their parents' perceptions of the estate, the children learnt to use several important techniques of collecting and presenting information and ideas.

A Mixed Farm

Most practical work concerned with developing children's spatial ability will necessarily take place in the immediate environment of the school. There are some schools, however, which give children experience of doing such work away from the school in a residential setting. This work may form part of a wider environmental experience, within or outside an integrated curriculum. One such scheme is 'Farms for City Children', an educational charity which enables children from urban primary schools to spend a week living and working on Parsonage Farm, a mixed farm near Hatherleigh in North Devon. This farm now combines Rectory Farm and Bridge Town shown on the map in Figure 4.3. The land covers most of the area to the north and east of the rivers in the model in Figure 4.5 and part of it is shown in the photograph in Figure 4.7.

A great deal of preparation precedes a visit to the farm. Children draw a map of England showing the position of Devon in relation to their home town, and insert on it their route, measuring distance and indicating the direction of travel. On a larger scale map of Devon they show the location of Parsonage Farm between the town of Hatherleigh and village of Iddesleigh a few miles north of Dartmoor. They learn about the types of farming practised in north Devon and the influence of weather, climate, land and soil on farming. They also acquire a working knowledge of farming routine and the main types of livestock and crops. Their vocabulary is enlarged to include technical terms such as drainage, fertiliser and grass leys.

The children also have to understand the farm as a working unit in which the farmer grows crops and manages livestock for an economic return. The farm is conceived as a simple system with a number of interrelated elements. The inputs include rain, sunshine, soil, fertiliser, the labour of the farmer and his workers and, in the initial stages, the stock of animals and seed for crops. At the heart of the system is the plant, consisting of the farm buildings, equipment and machinery. The output comprises all the products that provide the farmer with income, such as milk, grain, calves, lambs and poultry for sale.

Parsonage Farm covers an area of some 300 acres and most of the land consists of pasture used for grazing cattle and sheep. There are 40 milking cows (Friesians, Jerseys and Guernseys), 50 assorted beef cattle, heifers and calves folks (Friesians, Devons and Herefords), 225 sheep (mostly there and Border Leicesters), and also 5 horses. In addition as a are 50 pigs, 20 hens and a few ducks and geese, a own and sheep dog and several cats. Fodder crops are al the year a day-by-day account of work on the farm throu 79) which is contained in an illustrated volume (Morpur describes in detail the farm as an economic u d their

Into this setting come about 35 chil large country teachers each week during term. They st totally mansion, Nethercott House, on the farm the complete immersed in the life and work of the

week. The main aim is to give children experience of farming
and this takes precedence over all other activities. The
children have to get up early and before breakfast some are in
the dairy whilst the cows are being milked, and others are
feeding the pigs. After breakfast the children return to the
dairy to wash it down and muck out the yard whilst the others
go to feed the cattle and horses in the fields in summer and
in the barns in winter. The sheep also have to be counted and
checked in the fields to ensure that none is missing, lame or
in need of attention. Other children feed the poultry, collect
the eggs, and groom the horses. After lunch special tasks may
be undertaken on the farm, such as cleaning out barns, shifting
bales of hay and straw, and planting saplings. Following
afternoon tea the children are once again in the dairy whilst
the cows are being milked, or feeding the pigs and any other
stock indoors before shutting up the barns for the night.

This busy schedule, in which children who have not been
on a farm before are totally preoccupied with farming, might
appear to leave little time for anything else. In spite of
the full programme of physical activity, however, it is possible for children to carry out a number of tasks aimed at
developing their spatial ability. The following is an account
of the exercises which were incorporated into the activities
of the same class of 35 children from Chivenor Primary School,
Birmingham, which carried out the study of the housing estate
described in the previous section.

Soon after arrival the children had to draw a plan of the
outside of Nethercott House during their 'free' time of two
hours at the end of the first or second morning. This was
done in a similar manner to the plan of the classroom which
had been drawn at school during the previous month. A scale
of 1:100 was used, thus permitting rapid and easy transformation of 1 metre on the ground to 1 cm on squared metric
paper. The house is an unusual shape, with several projections
and recesses, but by starting in one corner and working
round the building with 10 metre measuring tapes the children
were able to complete the measurements and transfer them to a
double sheet of paper within the time available. They also
drew field sketches of the house from the lawn in front of it.

A further exercise was carried out in the nearby village
of Iddesleigh. The children were provided with a map of the
buildings. The village on a scale of 1:1,250 (50 inches to
one mile). After a visit to the church and village hall,
formerly the school, at the western end of the village, the
children were able to orientate themselves as most of the
buildings lay to north of the west-east trending road.
Against each building shown on the map the children inserted
a letter and number. The letter indicated the materials of

which the walls were built: B for brick, S for stone, T for timber. The number showed the roofing material: 1 for slate, 2 for tiles, 3 for thatch. A photograph taken from the top of the church tower at the western end of the village showed the complete layout in a similar manner to a very low oblique air photograph. As such it constituted a useful record of the three-dimensional representation of buildings alongside the two-dimensional map. Annotated sketches of selected buildings drawn by the children provided a record of the ground-level viewpoint.

The biggest exercise completed by the children during the week was a land use map of Parsonage Farm. The 1:10,560 (6 inches to one mile) map formed the base map (Figure 4.3). The children visited the fields in turn on different days. On their base map they indicated the land use by means of a simple key: G for grass, R for rough pasture, A for arable, C for coniferous trees, D for deciduous trees, U for underwood and O for orchard. In practice only a few of the fields could be visited within any two-hour period, but during the week the land use map of the farm was built up. In the process the children learnt to orientate themselves and this was helped by the fact that most of their outward journeys were from the southern part of the map towards the north.

Incorporated into this exercise was another in which the children had to show symbolically whether the boundaries of each field consisted of hedges, fences or walls. The hedges between one or two fields had recently been taken up to create larger fields. The map was thus updated by removing from it these boundaries, which could be detected as slight depressions in the ground.

A further task was to mark on the map the direction of the slope of the land downwards by means of an arrow. In some fields more than one arrow was necessary, but the general trend of the slope down towards the rivers and streams was clearly discernible on the ground and could be marked on the map. The children were thus able to compare their representation of valleys and hills with the contour patterns on the map.

The final task in each field was to measure the angle of slope, using an Invicta clinometer, a cheap, simple and easily used device. Children worked in pairs, one standing at the highest point of the field and the other at the lowest point. The child at the higher point held the clinometer like a target pistol with arm outstretched, pointing it at the head of the other child. When the rotating, weighted and graduated disc became stationary, the trigger was released, holding the graduated disc in position, so that the angle could be read.

This enabled the children to appreciate the true meaning of a 5 or 10 degree slope.

These exercises on Parsonage Farm were part of an environmental studies curriculum. All were carried out in addition to the routine of physical work on the farm which occupied the children for much of each day. The orientation of the map out of doors, the location of fields and recording of land use and slope all helped to develop the children's spatial awareness of the farm as a unit. Knowledge and skills which the children had learnt at school were subsequently applied in the field in a setting which was new to them.

A Landscape Simulation

The development of skills involving the study and use of maps are regarded as important objectives of fieldwork for pupils in the 14-16 age range. Teachers attach considerable importance to such skills as the ability to orientate a map in the field, to follow a route using a map and to relate landforms to the contour patterns by which they are represented on a map (Boardman, 1974). Fieldwork for CSE and O-level usually takes the form of a course, consisting either of several days at a residential centre or an equivalent number of days spaced throughout the year. The Geography for the Young School Leaver and Geography 14-18 projects, however, both require pupils to undertake individual studies using an approach which involves the identification of a problem, definition of the objectives of an investigation and decisions about the evidence that is relevant and how to collect it. Subsequently pupils have to collect and record the evidence, analyse and interpret it, and reach conclusions in relation to the original objectives of the investigation, as described in Chapter 5. The fieldwork which is outlined here is based on a problem-orientated field course undertaken with fourth year pupils of average ability in a mixed comprehensive school (Boardman, 1979).

The four-day residential course took place in the Edale-Castleton area of Derbyshire shown on the maps in Figures 5.1 and 5.2 and the photograph in Figure 5.3. The entire course focused on a single problem: whether the Vale of Edale would form a suitable site for a reservoir, taking into account both environmental and social factors. The pupils had to decide what information to collect in order to solve the problem. Maps that were used in the field included the 1:10,560 Ordnance Survey maps of the Vale of Edale, the 1:25,000 map of the Edale-Castleton area, the 1:25,000 geological map produced for this area of special geological interest and the 1:63,360 Peak District tourist map which shows relief by means of layer colouring and hill shading as

well as contours. The pupils were also provided with a
duplicated outline map showing the location and extent of the
proposed reservoir and the sites that were to be visited
(Figure 7.1). All of the fieldwork was carried out from roads
and footpaths and, in order to avoid disturbing residents or
troubling visitors to a popular part of the National Park,
neither interviews nor questionnaires were used. The land
that would be flooded is shown in the photograph (Figure 7.2)
which was taken from above the site of the proposed dam
looking westwards.

The pupils were introduced to map reading in hilly
country on the afternoon of the first day when they followed
the footpath along the northern side of the valley from Edale
Youth Hostel (1 on Figure 7.1) eastwards to the top of the
ridge (2) separating the Vale of Edale from the neighbouring
Upper Derwent Valley. This valley once had the same characteristics as the Vale of Edale, but the land has been submerged
beneath the water of three huge reservoirs. The lower slopes
of the valley have been planted with coniferous woodland and
only the higher land remains as open moorland. From the viewpoint on the ridge the pupils had to consider whether an art-
ificial body of water is an intrusion on the landscape or
whether it might be regarded as an attractive addition to it.
They had to consider whether the slopes planted with coniferous trees in straight lines form an unnatural feature
of the landscape. The pupils then took the footpath down to
the site of the proposed dam (3) and on the return journey
walked along the road and near to the railway that would have
to be realigned, and recorded on base maps the farm land and
buildings that would be flooded. Follow-up work in the
evening included measurement of the lengths of road and railway that would have to be rebuilt and planning of alternative
routes for them.

Measurement of river flow undertaken on the upper reaches
of the River Noe at the head of the Vale of Edale (4)
provided the pupils with practice in the use of techniques
and demonstrated the way in which a scientific survey of a
catchment area would be completed by a water authority. Peb-
bles were taken out of the river and sorted into three types:
shale, fine-grained grit and coarse-grained grit. The river
was then followed upstream until out-crops of the grits could
be detected on the slopes of Kinder Scout, the impervious
Millstone Grit moorland gathering grounds of the tributaries
flowing into the valley below. On the return journey this
rock was compared with the crumbly Edale Shales into which
the valley has been cut (5). In the evening the pupils used
squared paper to calculate the area of land that would be
flooded by the proposed reservoir.

137

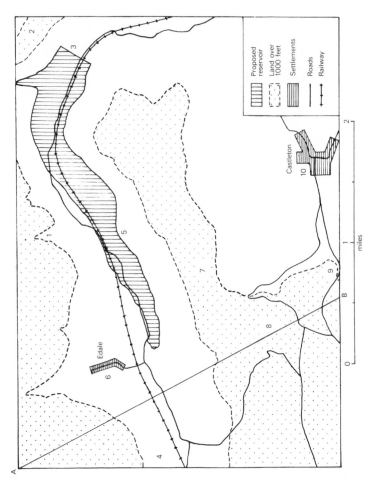

FIGURE 7.1. LOCATION OF PROPOSED RESERVOIR

FIGURE 7.2. PHOTOGRAPH OF RESERVOIR SITE

The pupils carried out a transect from north to south across the Vale of Edale approximately along the line AB in Figure 7.1. They used a large scale base map to study the village of Edale (6) and record the features that make it an attractive place for visitors and the kind of provision made for them. They recorded land use on a transect diagram as they crossed the valley, climbed on to the ridge on its southern side (7), a good point from which to view the Vale, and thence reached the top of Mam Tor (8). During the follow-up work in the evening the pupils had to make a plan for the recreational use of the proposed reservoir and its valley. Thus they inserted on outline maps such features as viewpoints, picnic and camp sites, and sailing, canoeing and fishing areas. They also had to decide the levels to which the slopes could be planted with trees and indicate possible locations of short walks and nature trails and routes for pony trekking.

The pupils spent one morning completing the transect by studying the Carboniferous Limestone landscape south of Mam Tor. The influence of geology on the choice of a site for a reservoir was illustrated by Winnats Pass, a narrow, steep sided but dry valley (9). The traffic scheme which closes the road through the valley to vehicles at weekends during the summer was discussed in the light of the increase in tourism which would probably take place if the Vale of Edale were to be further developed. A visit to one of the caves and the village of Castleton (10) illustrated the importance of tourism in the area and completed the site visits.

Subsequent work involved preparation for a simulation of a public enquiry on the proposal to construct the reservoir. The pupils suggested the kinds of people who might support or object to the scheme. Supporters would probably include the water authority, a leisure amenities firm, a group of Sheffield industrialists, local licensees of public houses, and the Youth Hostel Association. Objectors would probably include local farmers, village residents, ramblers, naturalists and the Peak Park Planning Board. Numerous resources produced by the Board were made available to the pupils, who then had to assume the roles of different people. They needed time in which to search through these resources and prepare the roles assigned to them.

Each pupil had to write a letter expressing his or her views on the proposed scheme to the Inspector who would conduct the public enquiry. Thus the water authority would point to the increasing demand for water and to the fact that one-third of the area of the Peak District National Park forms gathering grounds for reservoirs, 48 already being in existence within the Park's boundaries. The leisure amenities firm would argue for the need to provide recreational activities for people in the urban areas surrounding the Park, and would emphasise the economic benefits of tourism to the local community.

On the other hand a farmer would object strongly to the loss of farm buildings and best land by flooding and also to the severing of farm land on the two sides of the valley, thereby destroying an effective working unit. A rambler would object to the increased pressure on the resources of the valley if the reservoir were used for recreational purposes and a naturalist to the detrimental effect of planting trees on the valley sides, thereby disturbing the wildlife habitats.

The letters provide the basis for the presentation of arguments for and against the proposal at the public enquiry. Simulation promotes purposeful activity, is problem based, lends itself to interdisciplinary enquiry, and is dynamic because it deals with a changing situation (Taylor and Walford, 1972). The management of a simulation requires careful organisation, however, if the full involvement of the pupils is to be obtained. A rehearsal may be desirable before the actual enquiry is held in order to familiarise pupils with the procedures. If they have not previously participated in a simulation pupils may not find it easy to step into other people's shoes and appreciate the attitudes of different people to a proposed scheme. They may need practice in speaking to an audience and showing maps and sketches. The pupils may present their arguments with the teacher acting as chairman of a public enquiry which involves the whole class. Alternatively the class may be divided into groups of six or eight with a pupil as chairman. In either case the enquiry should be followed up with written work. Pupils might write a report of the proceedings for the local newspaper, or present a report in the form in which it might be written by the Inspector who conducts the enquiry.

Similar material for a simulation of this kind could be gathered through fieldwork in any upland area where relief and geology indicate a potential site for a reservoir. It is one way of providing a problem-orientated focus for fieldwork and at the same time combining physical and human geography. It also forms the basis of the kind of work recommended for individual studies by both the Geography for the Young School Leaver and the Geography 14-18 projects. A landscape model of an area in which fieldwork has been undertaken could be constructed and submitted for assessment in addition to a report illustrated with maps, sketches and photographs. Examination requirements apart, however, this type of study makes a valuable contribution to the pupils' environmental education. It should help pupils to develop an appreciation of the quality of the landscape in rural areas and cultivate attitudes to problems of the conservation of the environment.

A Planning Problem

Since young people have the right to vote in national and
local government elections at the age of 18 it is appropriate
to make them aware of the importance of decision making procedures. Indeed it seems essential that students undertaking
advanced studies should have opportunities to practise decision
making during their courses and thus develop the ability to
make reasoned decisions in the adult world. Students should
also be asked to justify their decisions after taking into
account all necessary considerations.

   Local planning problems provide useful case study material
and require an understanding of local government planning,
public consultation and decision making procedures. Their use
is recommended by the Geography 16-19 project as one form of
enquiry based learning. The worked example which is given
below follows the route for enquiry advocated by the project
for students in this age range, as described in Chapter 6.
This begins with the identification of a question, problem or
issue, followed by observation and perception using fieldwork
and resource material. Subsequently definition and description
direct the students towards analysis and explanation. Finally
evaluation and prediction lead to decision making and recom-
mendations. All of the events which are described below
actually took place in the Birmingham suburb of Harborne
during 1981. They show the relevance of geographical enquiry
to planning problems in the modern world.

   Harborne lies three miles to the south-west of the centre
of Birmingham, at a point where a busy radial road to the city
boundary intersects the outer ring road. This intersection,
known as Prince's Corner, marks the historic focus of the old
village of Harborne when it began to develop in the late
eighteenth and early nineteenth centuries out of a small rural
community with a parish church. Prince's Corner was the site
of the village green on which were held communal festivals
such as fairs, and in the buildings grouped around the green
were found most of the village shops. During the second half
of the nineteenth century, ribbon development along the radial
road, the construction of a railway with a station in Harborne,
and the official incorporation of the village into the city,
changed the character of Harborne into that of a dormitory
suburb for Birmingham. Today Prince's Corner retains some
notable buildings, including an attractive purpose-built row
of Victorian shops in sound condition and two public houses.

The road intersection, however, is also a traffic bottle-
neck, particularly in the morning and evening rush hours.
Traffic converges on a small roundabout from four directions,
and because the junction is staggered, right turns have to be
negotiated even by traffic following the ring road. The West
Midlands County Council, as the body responsible for highways,
announced in March 1981 a road improvement scheme by which the
outer ring road south of Prince's Corner would be widened from
a single to dual carriageway. The present road, Harborne Park
Road, is shown near the lower edge of the aerial photograph in
Figure 4.9 and the map in Figure 4.10. Part of Prince's
Corner can be seen on the extreme left of the photograph and
the end of an existing dual carriageway on the right. The
City Planning Department, as the body responsible for local
plans, incorporated the scheme into its draft local plan which
was published in April 1981. Few details were revealed except
for a map and display in the local library for three weeks in
May 1981. The map (Figure 7.3) shows that the County's road
widening scheme would involve the demolition of more than 50
properties, including all the shops on Prince's Corner, the
removal of the small roundabout and its replacement by traffic
lights. At a public meeting held in the local church hall on
10 June 1981 strong opposition was voiced to the scheme.
Objections were raised on social, economic and environmental
grounds. Members of the public protested that the historic
centre of Harborne village would almost completely disappear.
The County plan would bring about the effective destruction of
the community focus at Prince's Corner. The proposed road
would truncate the community, separating customers from their
shops and children from their schools, and the greater volume
and faster speed of traffic on the ring road would increase
the danger to pedestrians. Old established and popular local
shops would be demolished and the closure of businesses would
create unemployment among local people. Some of the older and
more interesting buildings would be pulled down in spite of
their good condition, and much needed housing would also be
demolished. Even before the demolition began, planning blight
on many properties would result in a progressive deterioriation
of the area as a commercial and residential centre. The
County's proposed scheme would be extremely expensive at a
time when financial resources are scarce.

The Harborne Society subsequently undertook its own
investigation of the problem and produced a 25-page report on
the future of Prince's Corner in September 1981. This report
questioned the need for a major improvement scheme and compared
traffic census figures collected by the West Midlands County
Council on 10 February 1981 with those collected nearly three
years previously on 20 June 1978. The County Surveyor's
estimated figures for 1991, calculated using a mathematically
based formula, were supplied in a letter to the Harborne

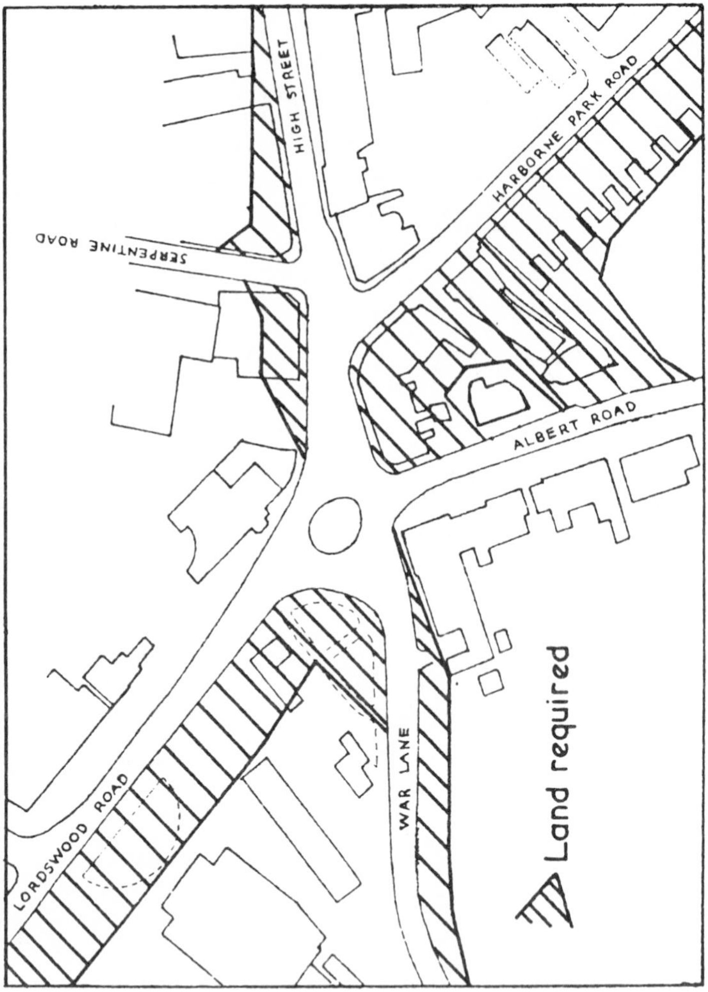

FIGURE 7.3. MAP OF COUNTY COUNCIL ROAD SCHEME

Society on 22 July 1981. The three sets of figures deserve
close scrutiny and are reproduced in the following table:

TABLE 7.1. TRAFFIC CENSUS FIGURES AT PRINCE'S CORNER, HARBORNE

	1978 v/h	1981 v/h	% Change 1978-81	1991 v/h	% Change 1981-91
Lordswood Road	2115	1618	− 23%	2728	+ 68%
War Lane	805	783	− 3%	1718	+119%
Harborne Park Road	926	966	+ 4%	1913	+ 98%
High Street	1622	1228	− 24%	2011	+ 64%
Total	5468	4595	− 16%	8370	+ 82%

Time 0800 − 0900 hours

v/h vehicles per hour

It will be seen that the actual figures for 1978 and 1981,
far from showing an overall increase in the traffic using
Prince's Corner, reveal an actual decrease of 16%. On what
grounds, therefore, did the County Surveyor reverse this down-
ward trend and predict an overall increase of 82% in the
traffic by 1991? The Harborne Society argued that there was
unlikely to be much change in the 1981 figures during the
decade for a number of reasons. It was doubtful whether there
would be any significant increase in the general level of car
ownership, particularly as unemployment remained at a high
level and car running costs continued to rise. Futhermore,
the West Midlands County Council was pursuing a policy of
reduced fares on buses to encourage more people to use public
transport. Traffic on the Birmingham outer ring road was
likely to be reduced still further when the motorway 'box'
around the city was completed after the construction of the
southern M42 link between the M5 and M6.

Fieldwork and site visits indicated that there were three
main causes of traffic congestion at the intersection. One was
the volume of traffic turning right because of the staggered
nature of the junction. A second was the siting of pedestrian
crossings at the junction, with considerable and random
restriction of traffic flow. A third was the siting of bus
stops at and near the intersection, thus restricting entry to
and exit from the roundabout to a single lane. These observations, together with the traffic census figures, indicated
that low level traffic management measures were called for
rather than large scale road reconstruction.

145

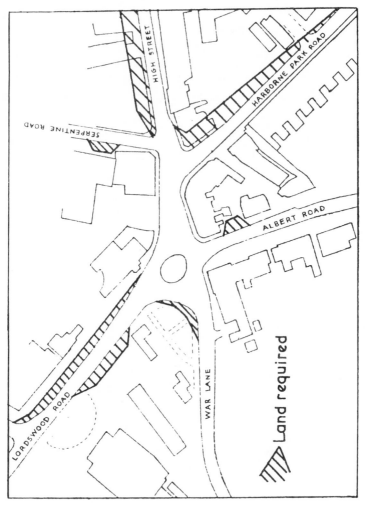

FIGURE 7.4. MAP OF LOCAL SOCIETY ROAD SCHEME

An alternative scheme was therefore proposed by the Harborne Society (Figure 7.4). This was essentially an ordinary crossroads - type of intersection controlled by traffic lights. Only one building, a public house on the corner of the High Street and Harborne Park Road, would have to be demolished and this land, together with small parcels of other vacant land, would provide a sufficiently wide carriageway for two lanes of traffic waiting at traffic lights on all four roads and single lanes for traffic leaving the junction on all four roads. The lights would have an all-red phase to allow pedestrians to cross but, because of the shorter distances across roads, the time phase would be shorter. All buses would stop in laybys near to the intersection, thus permitting the uninterrupted flow of other traffic.

The Society acknowledged that vehicle speeds would be slower and journey times longer than those which the County plan would achieve, but argued that this consideration was outweighed by the numerous advantages of their alternative scheme. The architectural and historical heritage of the neighbourhood would be protected and the community would preserve as much as possible of its village character. Planning blight on some fifty properties would be obviated and local shops and businesses would be retained. The existing and anticipated traffic flow would be within the capacity of the proposed system of traffic signals. The provision of laybys for all bus stops would not only improve traffic flow but would facilitate the use and movement of buses. The use of conventional traffic signals would cause minimal disruption to traffic and community life during installation. The cost of the proposed scheme would be only a fraction of that of the County scheme. The Harborne Society supported its case not only with maps and photographs but also a sketch showing Prince's Corner as it looks at present (Figure 7.5) and another sketch showing the dramatic change that would be brought about by the County's scheme (Figure 7.6).

Which of these two schemes should be implemented? Should the movement of traffic take precedence over the preservation of a site of historical, social and economic importance? These are the kinds of questions which a student would have to consider in undertaking a study of a local planning problem. Clearly a decision on an issue such as that discussed in this section would be made only after a detailed investigation of the local area involving a sympathetic appreciation of the significance of the proposal. Planning is directly concerned with the environment and planning decisions can have a profound impact on the lives of members of the public. Students who become involved in local planning issues acquire a concern for the urban environment and an ability to participate in making decisions about its future.

FIGURE 7.5. SKETCH OF PRINCE'S CORNER AS IT IS

FIGURE 7.6. SKETCH OF PRINCE'S CORNER AS IT MIGHT BE

8   Computers and Graphicacy

The computer is playing an increasingly prominent role in
learning in a technological age. Eventually it will probably
be as commonplace as the electronic pocket calculator.
Computer assisted learning can be used by geography teachers
in a variety of ways as a means of developing graphicacy. It
can help pupils to master knowledge and practical skills
through drill and practice routines. It can enhance understanding by simulating a process or sequence of events so
that concepts and variables are better appreciated. The computer can perform rapid calculations and analyse data speedily,
thus saving time and increasing motivation in the classroom.
Data storage, retrieval and analysis facilities can be
utilised for the purposes of comparing and contrasting several
sets of information.

Skill Practice

It is possible for the teacher to use the computer as an
'electronic blackboard' to demonstrate geographical ideas or
processes to an assembled class. Video signals of screen
displays can be relayed to one or more large screen television
monitors installed at prominent places in the classroom, thus
permitting all members of a class to see the displays.
Instead of looking at static blackboard maps or overhead
projector maps and diagrams, students can watch animated displays of geographical processes, such as the growth of a city.
Pupils are passive recipients of information or ideas when
watching television monitors in this way, however, and they
derive greater benefit from interacting personally with the
computer.

Practice is provided in two essential skills for the
effective use of Ordnance Survey maps, grid references and
compass directions, by means of a computer program called Hunt
the Hurkle (Shepherd, 1976). The program can be used with
first year secondary school pupils who are mastering these

basic skills or with older pupils who need periodic revision
in giving locational co-ordinates. It is a good program for
introducing newcomers to the use of the computer because of
the simplicity of its operation, its high motivational appeal,
its recreational quality, and the practical, everyday use of
the skills in which it provides practice.

The hurkle is an imaginary animal which hides itself at
random in a square shaped area on the screen. The aim of the
exercise is to try and locate the hurkle in a specified number
of guesses, helped by the directional clues provided in the
program. The pupil has to guess where the hurkle is hiding
and type in grid references consisting of two, four or six
figures, depending upon his level of familiarity in using co-
ordinates. The grid references in the square shaped area are
based on a point of origin at its south-west corner. Eastings
have to be typed in before northings and, for the purposes of
clarity, a comma is typed in to separate the two numbers.
Thus the south-west corner of the square has the grid reference
0, 0. A two figure grid reference 5, 8 would be a point 5
distance units to the east of the origin and 8 distance units
to its north. The eastings and northings run from 0 to 9 for
two-figure grid references, from 00 to 99 for four figures,
and from 000 to 999 for six figures. The similarity of this
procedure to that recommended for teaching grid references in
Chapter 3 will be immediately apparent.

When the pupil has made an initial guess at the location
of the hurkle, the computer will respond with an instruction to
go in a certain direction, such as south-east or north-west.
The directional clues given by the computer use only the eight
principal points of the compass. Guessing should be confined
to the first attempt, therefore, and the pupil's subsequent
attempts should make use of the directional clues provided.
The computer allows only a limited number of attempts to locate
the hurkle before it terminates the round and reveals the
location. Five attempts are permitted with two figure grid
references, ten with four figures, and fifteen with six figures.
If the pupil succeeds in locating the hurkle within the maximum permitted number of attempts, the computer responds with
a message of congratulations. If the pupil is unsuccessful,
the computer offers another chance to hunt the hurkle, which
hides in another random location in the area. Pupils can
continue to practise at the computer until they feel that their
skill has improved. They can progress from two figure grid
references to four figures and six figures when they feel ready
to do so. There is no change in the principle of the exercise
when graduating to four or six figures; the pupils merely have
to think about more precise locations with each successive
increase in the digits.

If pupils are to make the most effective use of their
practice time on the computer they should be encouraged to
develop a systematic approach to discovering where they made
errors in an unsuccessful run. This highlights the use of the
computer as an aid to learning. The teacher continues to play
an important role; with this particular exercise his function
is to identify potentially weak pupils and give them additional
guidance. Pupils experiencing difficulty or making mistakes
could, for example, take to the computer a piece of paper
ruled in the form of a gridded square area. They record their
progress at each attempt by marking on the paper a numbered
cross to represent each attempt and the grid reference, followed by an arrow to show the direction indicated by the
computer. This recording not only reduces possible confusion
between eastings and northings, but also encourages clear
thinking. For example, the pupil's initial guess might be 4,
6 to which the computer replies 'go north-east'. This suggests
that the hurkle is hiding somewhere in the north-east of the
area. The pupil types in 8, 9, and the computer responds 'go
south-west', implying that the hurkle is not in the extreme
north-east corner. The pupil types in 7, 8 and the computer
says 'go west', indicating that, while the northing is probably
correct, the value of the easting needs to be reduced.
Accordingly the pupil tries 6, 8 and this elicits from the
computer 'Congratulations! You found it in 4 guesses'.

If pupils fail to find the hurkle in the permitted number
of moves, the reason is probably either that they give the
eastings and northings in the wrong order, or that they do not
relate the directional clues provided by the computer to an
appropriate increase or decrease in the numerical values of
the two co-ordinates. In this case the teacher should direct
the pupils to check their progress grids against the computer
printouts. Thus, in the example already given, the pupil
might type in the first three moves: 4, 6; 8, 9; 7, 8. At the
fourth attempt, however, the pupil may confuse eastings and
northings, typing in 8, 6. In other words, instead of going
west he goes south-east, even though he may have guessed the
correct location mentally. Backtracking through a sequence of
moves in this way not only helps to identify errors but is
also further practice at plotting points and using direction.

The teacher will see that, if the pupil uses a sensible,
systematic approach, the hurkle can usually be located within
the permitted number of attempts. The secret of the strategy
is to narrow down the area of search systematically. This is
best done by starting the search at or near the centre of the
area and subsequently moving to the centre of the quarter
indicated by the computer's directional clues. Thus in the
example given, after the initial guess 4, 6 and the clue 'go
north-east', the pupil's move could have been 6, 7. The next

clue would have been 'go north', thus indicating the correct
move, keeping the easting constant, to be 6, 8. Since the
adoption of this strategy may reduce the challenge of hunting
the hurkle, it is probably best for pupils to discover it for
themselves. With slower pupils, however, the teacher may
decide to reveal the strategy to assist them in their search
once they have thoroughly mastered the giving of grid references and are responding to directional clues correctly. It
will be apparent that the Hunt the Hurkle program combines
high motivational appeal with considerable practice in two
basic map reading skills. The pupil is engaged in interactive
work with the computer. It would be impossible for the teacher
to provide this kind of practice individually with a class of
thirty pupils. But the teacher retains the responsibility for
teaching grid references and direction; the computer only
provides the practice.

In an adaptation of the program used by Fox (1981) with
second year mixed ability pupils, the teacher tells the class
that a murderer is at large in a 10 km by 10 km square of a
1:50,000 Ordnance Survey map. The pupils trace their own grid
from the map and play the role of the police in catching the
murderer. When a pupil has chosen the starting point for the
search, the four figure grid reference is typed into the computer and the pupils mark it on their own grids. The computer
then gives a 'tip-off' about the location of the hiding
murderer (e.g. 'go south'). The pupils delimit on their own
maps the area where they think the murderer may be found and
block all roads and footpaths in pencil on the tracing paper
over their maps. Another pupil types a four figure grid reference into the computer, to which it again responds (e.g. 'go
east'). The pupils delimit this new smaller area and close in
on the murderer. The exercise is repeated until the pupils
find the grid square in which the murderer's hiding place is
located. The pupils then examine the grid square on the
Ordnance Survey map and make a list of possible hideouts.

Simulation Games

In geographical games the computer performs calculations
rapidly and enables pupils to see the results of their
decisions. A version of the farm game devised by Tidswell
(1972) is available as a program in the geography pack
produced by the Schools Council Computers in the Curriculum
project (Schools Council, 1979). The game is one of eight
programs supported by documentation in A4 size loose-leaf
sheets consisting of teacher's notes and pupils' leaflets or
worksheets which may be duplicated for class use without
permission.

The farm game can be played by pupils aged 10-13 in top primary, upper middle or lower secondary school classes. As in the manual version of the game, the players adopt the role of farmers and aim to obtain the highest average income by deciding on which combinations of crops to grow before they know the weather for the following season. The game shows the pupils that the farmer has to make decisions when he is uncertain about the weather, allows pupils to participate in making decisions, and illustrates the relationship between farming and weather.

The function of the computer is to overcome the main problem with the manual version of the game; that the pupils have to spend too much time making tedious calculations of crop yields and income with each combination of weather and crops. The computer also ensures complete accuracy in the calculations, in contrast to pupils who inevitably make errors which sometimes lead to confusing and unrealistic results. The random number generator in the computer program simulates the random variations in weather from year to year, replacing the chance cards in the manual version of the game. Use of a random factor on income, which allows for a latitude of plus or minus 5 per cent on calculated income, introduces a further element of realism by taking into account such variables as inflation, fluctuations in crop prices and extreme local variations in weather.

The players are provided with a map of a farm containing five fields of different sizes and totalling 135 hectares. They have to choose the crops to grow in each field, selecting from cereals (wheat, barley, oats), roots (sugar beet, potatoes), legumes (beans) and grass. They are given a table listing the growing costs and the income expected from each of the seven crops under four different weather conditions: warm and wet (broadly corresponding with south-west England), warm and dry (eastern England), cool and wet (western Scotland), and cool and dry (eastern Scotland). Pupils work out the estimated profit or loss per hectare for each crop under each type of weather. They are also provided with a table showing the probability of the four weather types occurring in different parts of Britain: thus in south-west England there is .5 probability that the weather will be warm and wet, .1 warm and dry, .3 cool and wet, and .1 cool and dry, whereas in eastern England the figures are .2, .4, .1 and .3 respectively.

After studying the information on field size, crop returns and weather possibilities, the pupils have to decide in which of three regions of Britain they want their farm to be situated, select the crops for each field for the first year, and then type them into the computer keyboard. The random number generator in the program indicates the type of weather for that

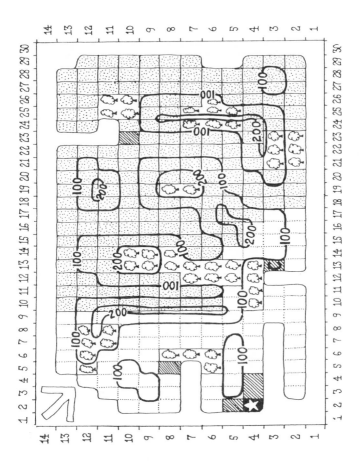

FIGURE 8.1. WINDMILL LOCATION GAME MAP

year. The computer then calculates the profit or loss on each field and gives the farmer's income. It does this for a sequence of four years and calculates the farmer's average income over that time. The pupils then reflect upon their success as farmers and compare their results with those of other members of the class. If they have been successful they can retain the same crops in the same fields, and the computer will calculate their income for a further four or eight years. If the pupils have been less successful, they can change the crops in any or all of the five fields. Having received new instructions, the computer performs further calculations of the profit or loss on each field, together with the farmer's income. Pupils should make notes of their reasons for the various choices of crop combinations and draw conclusions from the results obtained. They can also discuss some of the ways in which a farmer balances his need for the highest income in the long term with his wish to avoid getting into debt in the short term if there is a period of unfavourable weather.

The use of grid references and other map reading skills is incorporated into some other computer programs. A game requiring an understanding and interpretation of contour lines is the Windmill Location Game included in the geography pack of the Computers in the Curriculum Project (Schools Council, 1979). The pupils are provided with a contour map of a wheat-growing island and on it they select sites for windmills taking into account height, prevailing north-westerly wind, the distribution of wheat growing areas and proximity to woodland. All of these have to be considered in relation to the location of the market, since grain milling is a weight-loss industry, and transport costs to the market. The game is based on Weber's location theory, which states that the optimum (least cost) location of the processing plant (windmill) depends on the relative transport costs of the raw material (wheat) and finished product (flour). Whilst transport costs are usually calculated in proportion to distance, and the market is a fixed point, a bakery in a town on the south-west coast of the island, the source of the raw material extends over a large area of wheat farms occupying stippled rectangles on the game map (Figure 8.1). The flour milling industry is a useful basis for an industrial location game because it depends on one raw material (grain) and one finished product (flour) for transport to the market (bakery). It avoids the complicating factors that influence the modern pattern of industrial location in advanced economies where electricity is universally available as a source of power.

Before going to the computer the pupils are given two simple exercises to do. First, they are told that each wheat farm produces 20 bags of grain from which a miller can obtain 12 bags of flour. They are asked to consider a farm located

6 km from the town where the bakery is located. If it costs
1p to carry 1 bag for 1 km, how much less expensive is it to
have the grain turned into flour at a mill 1 km from the farm
than at a mill 1 km from the town? Clearly it is cheaper to
mill the flour near the farm. Second, the pupils are told
that the new mills will have auxiliary steam engines built in
to allow for inadequate wind power. Some sites will clearly
be better placed than others to make full use of the wind and
thus avoid using the expensive steam engines, which depend on
coal transported from the port at costs which are proportional
to distance between the port and each mill. How good are
sites at grid references 18, 12 and 26, 5? The former is a
good site near the top of a hillside facing the prevailing
wind, whilst the latter is a bad site on the sheltered side of
a hill and near woods which will obstruct the full force of
the wind.

Pupils then choose locations for six windmills and type
them into the computer, giving column numbers (eastings) before row numbers (northings). The computer responds with
three tables. The first shows how many bags of grain the
mill would receive and the number of days it would be powered
by wind and steam engine, on the assumption that each mill
could process five bags per day. Thus a mill located at 11,
13 on an open but low-lying site would receive 420 bags and
be powered by wind for 84 days, needing an engine for none,
whilst a mill located at 15, 7 on sheltered lowland would
receive 500 bags but would be powered by wind on only 55 days,
requiring an engine for a further 45 days. The second table
produced by the computer shows the cost of transport from
farms to mill and from mill to bakery, on the assumption that
both flour and grain are carried at a cost of 1p per bag per
km, but that it takes 20 bags of grain to make 12 bags of
flour. The third table lists running costs for each mill,
comprising transport costs, steam engine coal, miller's wages
(the same wherever they work) and rent (a small item, but less
on woodland sites than on farmland or near towns).

The computer then produces a map showing the area of
farms served by the mills at the six chosen sites, calculated
on the assumption that each farmer will take his grain to the
nearest mill. Pupils are asked to draw lines around the
farms served by each mill on their six-mill maps, and then
to draw arrows from each mill to the nearest town. They are
invited to compare their results with those obtained by other
members of the class. They should discuss the best pattern of
sites for six mills and explain their conclusions. Is it
better, for example, for the mills to be near a town, in a
wheat growing area, spread out over the island or clustered
together? Pupils who spread out their mill sites fairly

evenly across the wheat growing area, take into account local site factors and possibly give a slight bias towards the market where feasible, will achieve the best performance.

The computer thus relieves the pupils of the need to spend much time on purely arithmetical calculations and eliminates the associated errors that would almost inevitably occur. All the pupils have to do is to type into the keyboard the grid references of the selected sites. The computer performs all the cost calculations. The pupils immediately see the consequences of their choice and then have an opportunity to change unprofitable sites for new ones. The computer is assisting their learning of elementary industrial location theory.

Data Analysis

Data accessibility is often a major problem for teachers and students alike. The collection of data still has to be done manually and takes time even when material containing the required information is readily available. Census returns, for example, constitute a valuable source of data in geography but they are expensive to purchase and it takes time to extract the required data from copies in public libraries.

Problems of data collection, storage, retrieval and analysis have been tackled by the Computer Assisted Learning in Upper School Geography (CALUSG) project based at the University of Birmingham Faculty of Education from 1976 to 1979. This was one of two geography projects funded as part of the National Development Programme in Computer Assisted Learning, which altogether sponsored some thirty development projects, mainly in higher rather than secondary education, at a total cost of £3 million (Hooper, 1977). CALUSG developed a new computer package, Geographical Statistical Package (GSP), to store and analyse data collected from a number of published sources, such as census returns, hydrological tables and geology, soil and land utilisation maps.

The computer printouts take the form of data tables, diagrams, graphs and maps. These are linked to a student text and series of exercises which require the students to read and interpret information presented on the computer printouts. These computer generated materials have been published as a series of units in the form of A4 size student booklets on four themes   (Robinson, Boardman, Fenner and Blackburn, 1978, 1979). The publication of units in this way means that computer-generated material can be used by students in any school, since access to a computer is not required and no computing expertise is necessary on the part of either teacher or student.

FIGURE 8.2. COMPUTER MAP OF AFFLUENCE IN BIRMINGHAM

Measurements taken from the map of a single drainage basin in the manner described in Chapter 6 can be carried further by students by reference to units in the Drainage Basins theme. A unit on drainage density contains data for fifteen basins in England and Wales. The data include the total length of all stream channels in each basin, the area of the basin, and the drainage density. In addition the mean annual rainfall is provided for each basin, together with the rock type on which it lies. These data, presented both as tables and as graphs, enable students to examine relationships between drainage density and rainfall or drainage density and rock type. Mean stream discharge and seasonal variations in discharge are covered in other units, showing how the computer can be used to build a series of models by feeding into it data of varying degrees of refinement.

Maps can be produced on a computer using an appropriate mapping package such as SYMAP. This relieves students of most of the time consuming work involved in designing and drawing maps, although, as with other kinds of data analysis, it is useful for students to compile at least part of a map manually so that they understand the mechanics of its construction. Maps showing several different variables can be produced speedily by computer and permit the exploratory analysis of spatial data patterns.

The set of characters (letters, numbers and symbols) on the computer's lineprinter are used to draw the map. The varying tones of grey are produced by using characters and overprinting of graded visual density. Thus in the computer-generated choropleth map (SYMAP) showing affluence as measured by the percentage of households owning cars in the wards of Birmingham (Figure 8.2) the symbols −, + and O are used for the lowest three class intervals. The character O is over-printed with − for the next class interval. The densest shading is achieved by overprinting H, I, O and −. The use of characters in this way may result in a map of rather coarse appearance but the function of the map is to enable students to see quickly the main geographical distributions rather than the precise details about very small areas.

Computer-generated maps produced using census data enable students to make comparisons between different areas. Thus the units in the CALUSG Cities theme contain maps compiled from census data for four cities − London, Birmingham, Bristol and Liverpool. Data are tabulated, graphs plotted and maps drawn to show variations in population density, land value, accessibility, housing quality and affluence, the latter being derived from the percentage of households with cars. The intention is that students should compare patterns displayed in a map of one city with those in the corresponding maps of

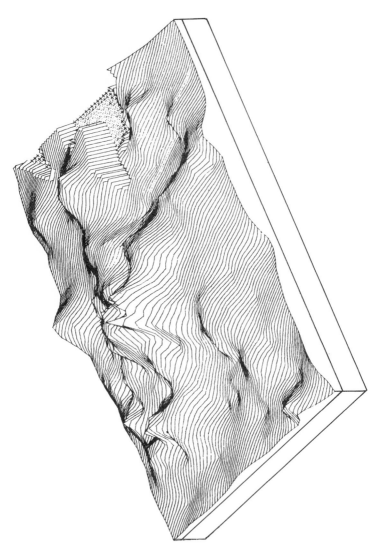

FIGURE 8.3. COMPUTER DIAGRAM OF JOURNEYS IN LONDON

other cities.

Data extracted from topographical, geology, soil and land
utilisation survey maps may be objectively compared in the
CALUSG Rural Landscapes theme. Each of four sample areas
(Cheddar, Exeter, Wendover, Snowdonia) covering an area 10 km
x 8 km is overlain by a grid of 975 rectangles. The altitude,
slope, rock type, soil type and land use are recorded for each
of these rectangles and stored. The computer performs the chi-
square test to ascertain whether there is a statistically
significant correlation between, for example, altitude and rock
type, or rock type and soil type, or soil type and land use.
This provides a more accurate statement of the spatial association between each pair of variables than can be obtained by
purely visual comparison. Thus in the sample area around
Cheddar (Figure 6.1) a positive spatial association is found
to exist between ground water gleys and riverine clays; gleyed
brown earths and Keuper Marl; and peaty gleyed podzols and Old
Red Sandstone.

Another computer package (SYMVU) transforms data on the
two-dimensional map into a three-dimensional block diagram.
In one example of this application the data fed into the computer consists of a series of grid references and the height
of the land at these points read from an Ordnance Survey map.
By interpolating from these heights the computer calculates
the height of points all over the map and thus produces a digital map. This base map is then used to generate perspective
views of the land surface in the form of three-dimensional
diagrams. These can be produced from different viewpoints
(such as from the north-west or the south-east), from different
angles above the horizon (such as 20 or 30 degrees), and with
various amounts of vertical exaggeration (such as x2 or x3).
The generation of this kind of block diagram is not confined
to data on topographical maps. Figure 8.3 shows the journey
to work pattern in Greater London derived from census data for
the boroughs processed with the SYMVU computer package for the
CALUSG People and Work theme.

Information about the views of teachers and reactions of
students to CALUSG units is available from the project evaluation (Boardman, 1977). Most teachers welcome them because they
provide types of data which are not readily accessible or would
take a long time to collect. The units also complement the
descriptive information contained in books, and the concrete
examples illustrate abstract generalisations. The practical
work involves the students actively in learning, providing a
change in teaching method. Teachers also recognise that the
units are relevant to modern A-level syllabuses and help to
prepare students for answering data response questions set in

examinations. Reservations expressed by teachers concern the amount of time needed to work through each unit and the quantity of paper resulting from the numerous computer print-outs. Difficulty is sometimes experienced in reading printouts because of the variable quality of lineprinting.

Student response to the units is also generally favourable. Most exercises are within the capabilities of the average sixth former, although there is a predictable variation in response among students representing a wide range of ability. In particular students seem to welcome being actively involved in working through practical exercises as a change from being given notes by the teacher or making notes from a book. The computer-produced data tables, graphs, maps and diagrams are initially rather confusing for some students and it takes them a little time to become accustomed to their novel appearance. Students with limited mathematical expertise also find the statistical techniques difficult to follow (Boardman and Robinson, 1979).

The CALUSG project units help to alleviate the shortage of readily accessible data and provide a means of analysing it. The project also brings to the attention of sixth form students and their teachers the potential of the computer for storing and analysing data, whilst the provision of structured exercises requires students to respond to the data. Although the project materials do not involve interaction between students and computers, they help to prepare the way for interactive work using other computer programs.

Microcomputers

The use of computers in the classroom is expanding rapidly. Teachers and students who have access to computer facilities (hardware) also require the appropriate computer programs (software). To facilitate the dissemination of programs suitable for schools the National Development Programme in Computer Assisted Learning supported the establishment of the Geographical Association Package Exchange (GAPE). This is based in the Geography Department of Loughborough University of Technology and is operated jointly under the auspices of the University and the Association.

The purpose of GAPE is to collect existing useful computer packages (programs plus educational and technical documentation) from various sources and draw their existence to the attention of geography teachers. GAPE relies on a small number of contributors of programs who have expertise in both computing and geography. These are modified where necessary and developed into packages with supporting documentation. The experience of GAPE shows that there is a demand for computer packages initially from a relatively small number of enthusiastic teachers. Demand grows as the packages become more widely known and their potential is appreciated.

A full account of the educational potential of the computer is contained in a book written by the organisers of GAPE (Shepherd, Cooper and Walker, 1980). For the teacher who is completely new to the computer there is an introductory discussion of computer assisted learning with explanations of the various technical terms. For the teacher who already uses the computer and wants to experiment with it there is a comprehensive survey of the various roles that the computer can play in geography. Practical issues arising in the use of CAL in the classroom are discussed and teachers are advised on the choice of packages, how to implement them, how to use programs and how to deal with some of the problems and pitfalls that may occur. Computer printouts, including maps, graphs and diagrams as well as records of students' interactive work, are included for the purposes of illustration.

Just as the large mechnical calculating machine has been replaced by the small electronic pocket calculator, so the giant mainframe computer has been superseded for many routine tasks by the small desk-top microcomputer. The widespread availability of microcomputers at relatively low cost is greatly increasing the potential of computer assisted learning. The main advantages of microcomputers lie in their low cost of purchase and maintenance, their robustness and reliability, and their portability, which enable them to be used in any room where there is a 13 amp power socket. Programs are available on cassette or disc systems. Cassette systems are cheap to purchase and maintain, easy to operate and robust. Disc systems are usually more sophisticated and offer greater facilities for storing and retrieving information, but are more expensive to produce and maintain. Microcomputers can perform a wide variety of tasks in geography and those with high resolution graphics allow programs to move beyond the processing of numbers to the processing of colour images, including maps, diagrams and graphs. New programs being produced are of good quality, adequately documented and readily available for use in schools on microcomputers such as the Research Machines 380Z, Pet and Apple.

The geography packages developed both by GAPE and by the Schools Council Computers in the Curriculum Project, originally designed for use on mainframe computers, have now been converted to run on microcomputers. GAPE has also developed a series of new packages which utilise the potential of graphics on the microcomputer. One package concerned with map reading skills is designed to teach pupils in the 11-13 age range the

163

concept of slope, its representation and its implications for
human activities. In this interactive program the pupils are
presented with information about slopes, transfer it to another
form, and suggest the effects of the slope upon various types
of transport. Thus they choose a slope and state it as a
percentage. The computer draws the slope and it appears on
the screen without any vertical exaggeration. The pupils are
next asked to select a form of transport. An animated image
of this form of transport then attempts to climb the slope.
In this way pupils are led to an understanding of the relationship between slope and various types of transport. The
program thus supplements and reinforces the methods of teaching
contours and relief discussed earlier, both in the classroom
(pages 59-69) and in the field (pages 135-6). It is also a
useful aid in teaching pupils to calculate gradients and to
appreciate their effect upon road and rail routes (pages 98-9).

Another program concerned with map interpretation is
designed to teach the spatial structure of towns and cities
to pupils in the 12-15 age range. Urban land use maps are
generally so complex that patterns of land use are difficult
to discern. The program enables pupils to analyse information
about urban land use patterns by examining one category of land
use at a time. The computer will display one age or land use
type in isolation from the rest. It will calculate the percentage of the urban area occupied by each age or land use
type. It will measure the distance of each age or land use
type from the city centre. It will also calculate measures
of dispersion for each type. Pupils are thus introduced to
spatial analysis by computer. The program can be used to
teach patterns of urban land use to pupils after they have
made a study of part of a city such as the housing estate
described previously (pages 128-32). It can also be used as
an introduction to more detailed fieldwork for individual
studies in examination courses.

There are two important questions that need to be asked
about computer assisted learning (Boardman, 1981b). The first
concerns the quality of learning. That the computer saves
time is beyond dispute. But in what ways does it help the
pupil to understand topics or master skills better than by
means of conventional teaching methods? Teachers who use the
computer are advised to examine each program carefully and
then evaluate it on the basis of close observation of pupils
at work on the computer. It is extremely difficult to
evaluate the effectiveness of learning through interactive work
at the computer because it usually forms only a relatively
small part of the learning of a particular topic, idea or
skill. It is virtually impossible to isolate what students
learn at the computer from what they learn in other parts of
lessons, or in their reading assignments and project work.

COMPUTERS AND GRAPHICACY

For these reasons it is best to evaluate the process of
learning rather than its outcomes (MacDonald, Atkin, Jenkins
and Kemmis, 1977). Much of the learning which takes place
should be of a higher order than simple recall or recognition
and may be broadly termed comprehension which engages students
in meaningful operations on the material that is presented to
them. Examples of this will be found in the kinds of learning
involved in the programs discussed earlier. The pupil who is
'hunting the hurkle' has to respond to each directional clue
from the computer by giving a further grid reference. The
pupil using a simulation game has to make decisions at the end
of each round and give further instructions to the computer.
The drainage basin morphometry program requires the student
not only to feed data into the computer but also to compare
the results obtained from different basins and interpret them.

The second question that has to be asked concerns the
cost of computer assisted learning. Since the educational
potential has to be evaluated in qualitative rather than
quantitative terms, it is equally difficult to assess the cost
of computer assisted learning compared with conventional
teaching methods. The computer nearly always results in
additional costs which may not be matched by benefits that
lend themselves to measurement (Fielden and Pearson, 1978). A
large amount of subjective judgement is therefore involved in
deciding whether the cost of the extra resources needed is
justified in the light of benefits to pupils.

The DES Microelectronics Education Programme (MEP),
launched by the Government in 1981 with £9 million in funds
administered by the Council for Education Technology, aims to
help schools to prepare pupils for life in a society in which
microelectronics are commonplace. The establishment of four-
teen regional information centres by MEP in partnership with
consortia of LEAs brings all schools within reach of the
necessary expertise which provides advice on the use of microcomputers and the development of programs. The Department of
Industry's matched funding scheme supplies half the cost of the
purchase of an approved model of microcomputer (Acorn or 380Z)
provided that the LEA or school pays the rest and that at
least two teachers are trained to use microcomputers. The
BBC computer literacy scheme, first televised in 1982 and
supported by course materials, introduces beginners of all
ages to the practical and intellectual challenge of computing
and to the wide range of practical applications of the microcomputer. The designation of 1982 as Information Technology
year provides national recognition of the changes in the
storage, transmission and transformation of information made
possible by the new technology.

The microcomputer will never, however, be a substitute for the teacher. Nor will it ever replace conventional teaching methods. The microcomputer should be regarded as a tool or teaching aid. Its strengths complement those of the teacher, who cannot calculate as quickly, nor recall such large amounts of data, nor give much time to individuals when faced with a large class of pupils. On the other hand the teacher is good at initiating discussion, flexible in the amount of direction given to classes, and perceptive in developing pupils' work. This kind of communication contrasts sharply with the rigid conventions which have to be followed in the interactions between microcomputers and their users. It is unlikely that computer programs will ever become lessons in themselves. Most require some teacher involvement either before or after the computer exercise. Realistic hardware provision and the availability of software makes it perfectly feasible for small groups of pupils to be left working with the machine, freeing the teacher to participate in other classroom activities. Teachers and pupils in the classrooms of tomorrow will use microcomputers alongside all the other resources for teaching and learning.

Appendix: Graphicacy Skills

The ages at which children should be able to achieve various
skills of graphicacy cannot be specified precisely because of
their different rates of intellectual development. Nevertheless the experience of teachers in the classroom, together
with research evidence and the requirements of public examinations, does make it possible to suggest tentatively the
approximate ages by which children of average ability should
normally be capable of acquiring various skills of graphicacy.
The 100 graphicacy skills listed in the following pages are
divided into groups to indicate those which should normally
be attainable by pupils ages 7, 9, 11, 13, 16 and 19 years
respectively. It should be emphasised, however, that the
skills listed for each age group remain tentative and the
scheme is not intended to be applied rigorously to all pupils
in all circumstances. Some pupils will master the various
skills at earlier ages than those suggested here; slow
learners will not attain them until much later.

5-7

By the age of 7 children should normally be able to:

1. Follow directions using left, right, forwards, in a circle, etc.
2. Describe the relative locations of objects using before, behind, in front of, to the left of, etc.
3. Sort objects by relative size and draw round them.
4. Sort objects by their shapes, such as squares, circles, etc. and draw round them.
5. Draw round life size objects such as coins, pencils, toys, etc. to show their shapes in plan form.
6. Draw routes between objects drawn, such as the path of an inaginary crawling insect.
7. Draw symbols to illustrate picture maps or imaginary maps.
8. Measure spaces between objects using hands or feet.

7-9

By the age of 9 children should normally be able to:

9. Plot the cardinal directions NESW.
10. Use a compass to find NESW in the school playground.
11. Draw a plan at a very large scale, such as a desk top with objects on it.
12. Measure from a large scale plan, such as a teacher-prepared plan of the classroom.
13. Insert in their approximate positions on the plan objects in the room, such as blackboard, cupboards.
14. Record around the plan features seen from the room, such as playground, trees.
15. Draw free-hand a map showing a simple route, such as the journey to school.
16. Make a simple model of part of the neighbourhood such as a row of shops.
17. Give locations in grid squares, such as A1, B3, etc. as on an A to Z road map.
18. Measure straight line distances between two points on an A to Z road map.
19. Draw some conventional symbols on an imaginary map and add a key.
20. Identify different countries shown on atlas maps.

GRAPHICACY SKILLS

9-11

By the age of 11 children should normally be able to:

21. Plot the sixteen points of the compass.
22. State bearings in degrees: 45, 90, 135, etc.
23. Indicate directions in the neighbourhood.
24. Align a map of the school and neighbourhood by means of compass and buildings, e.g. church, numbered houses.
25. Find directions and bearings using a compass.
26. Orientate a large scale map (1:1,250 or 1:2,500) using buildings as reference points.
27. Relate position on the ground to location on a large scale map.
28. Use grid lines to locate points.
29. Give four figure grid references using eastings and northings.
30. Draw a plan of the classroom and/or school building.
31. Identify and name rooms on a teacher-prepared plan of the school.
32. Make measurements on large scale maps of the local area (1:1,250 or 1:2,500 or 1:10,000).
33. Measure the straight line distance between two fixed points on maps of progressively smaller scales.
34. Measure the winding distance along roads between two fixed points on maps of progressively smaller scales.
35. Compare symbols for the same feature on maps of progressively smaller scales.
36. Realise that the degree of generalisation on maps increases with decreasing scale.
37. Appreciate that some symbols on smaller scale maps are disproportionate to the size of the objects they represent.
38. Identify features on a low level oblique aerial photograph of the local area.
39. Make a scale model of part of the local area showing roads and buildings.
40. Give locations on atlas maps using latitude and longitude.

II-13

By the age of 13 pupils should normally be able to:

41. Orientate a 1:25,000 or 1:50,000 map with aid of a compass and prominent features.
42. Give six figure grid references on 1:25,000 and 1:50,000 maps.
43. Measure straight line distances on 1:25,000 and 1:50,000 maps.
44. Measure winding distances on 1:25,000 and 1:50,000 maps.
45. Describe a route on a map from a statement giving directions and distances.
46. Follow a route on the ground using a map from a statement giving directions and distances.
47. Identify and draw conventional symbols used on 1:25,000 and 1:50,000 maps.
48. Compile a key to illustrate classified or grouped point, line and area features shown on 1:25,000 and 1:50,000 maps.
49. Mould a plasticine model and draw contours on it by immersing it in water at regular intervals.
50. Construct a layer model from a contour map and fill in the spaces between layers to complete a landscape model.
51. Read heights from contours on a map and estimate heights between contours.
52. Draw a section across the contours on a map.
53. Calculate the vertical exaggeration of a cross section.
54. Calculate the average gradient between two points on a map.
55. Calculate approximate areas on maps using superimposed grid squares.
56. Identify simple relief features from contour patterns, such as valley, spur, hill, ridge.
57. Draw and/or annotate a landscape sketch from a photograph.
58. Correlate an oblique aerial photograph with a large scale map of the local area.
59. Describe a landscape or townscape using combined evidence of map and photograph.
60. Extract information from thematic maps in an atlas, such as relief or population.

13-16

By the age of 16 pupils should normally be able to:

61. Generalise about the height of the land in a given area on a 1:25,000 or 1:50,000 map.
62. Identify the overall relief divisions of a landscape and describe specific features within them.
63. Describe the shape of selected slopes in terms of concave, convex, uniform.
64. Subdivide the area shown on a 1:25,000 or 1:50,000 map into drainage basins.
65. Describe the shapes of the valleys within a drainage basin.
66. Describe the nature and pattern of rivers or streams within a drainage basin.
67. Generalise about the location and distribution of settlements shown on a 1:25,000 or 1:50,000 map.
68. Describe the site, situation, form and function of small settlements shown on a 1:25,000 or 1:50,000 map.
69. Describe patterns of communication shown on a map in terms of type, density and direction.
70. Relate types and patterns of communication to relief and drainage.
71. Relate human activity to the physical environment shown on a map.
72. Compare the physical and human features shown in two different parts of a map.
73. Draw and annotate a sketch map to illustrate selected spatial information.
74. Draw and annotate a landscape or townscape sketch in the field.
75. Correlate features on an oblique aerial photograph with the corresponding features on a map.
76. Describe a scene using the combined evidence of map and aerial photograph.
77. Use the combined evidence of map and photograph to infer human activity in an area.
78. Construct a landscape model from a map and show selected features on it.
79. Relate information on a 1:25,000 or 1:50,000 map to information shown on a thematic map in an atlas.
80. Correlate information on two or more thematic maps in an atlas, such as relief and vegetation.

16 – 19

By the age of 19 students should normally be able to:

81. Identify patterns of relief on topographical maps and suggest the origins of landforms shown.
82. Identify patterns of drainage on topographical maps and suggest reasons for these patterns.
83. Designate stream orders on a map and calculate bifurcation ratios in a drainage basin.
84. Determine the area of a drainage basin on a map and calculate drainage density in the basin.
85. Read geology maps and relate rock strata to relief and drainage on topographical maps.
86. Read soil maps and relate soil associations to relief and drainage on topographical maps.
87. Identify land use patterns on land utilisation maps and suggest reasons for these patterns.
88. Relate rock strata on geology maps to soil associations on soil maps.
89. Relate land use patterns on land utilisation maps to relief and drainage on topographical maps.
90. Relate rock strata on geology maps to land use patterns on land utilisation maps.
91. Relate soil associations on soil maps to land use patterns on land utilisation maps.
92. Analyse a rural land use pattern with the aid of a theoretical model, e.g. Von Thunen.
93. Analyse an urban land use pattern with the aid of a theoretical model, e.g. Burgess.
94. Analyse data on maps using a sampling technique and determine the reliability of the results, e.g. standard error.
95. Analyse the distribution of settlements on a map using a statistical technique, e.g. nearest neighbour analysis.
96. Calculate statistical indices as measures of the relationship between specific variables on maps, e.g. correlation coefficient.
97. Apply statistical tests as measures of the relationship between specific variables on maps, e.g. chi-square.
98. Relate oblique aerial photographs to various types of maps in order to interpret features on them.
99. Relate vertical aerial photographs to various types of maps in order to interpret features on them.
100. Present spatial data as point, linear and aerial distributions on maps, e.g. dot, isopleth and choropleth maps.

Bibliography

BALCHIN, W.G.V. and COLEMAN, A.M. (1965) Graphicacy should be the Fourth Ace in the Pack, The Times Educational Supplement, 5 November.

BALCHIN, W.G.V. (1972) Graphicacy, Geography, vol.57, pt.3.

BALCHIN, W.G.V. and COLEMAN, A.M. (1973) Progress in Graphicacy, The Times Educational Supplement, 11 May.

BALCHIN, W.G.V. (1977) Replacing the Three R's with the Four Aces, The Times, 19 April.

BARRETT, M. (1979) Art Education: A Strategy for Course Design, Heinemann.

BARTZ, B.S. (1965) Map Design for Children, Field Enterprises Educational Corporation.

BARTZ, B.S. (1970) Maps in the Classroom, Journal of Geography, vol.69, no.1.

BEARD, R.M. (1969) An Outline of Piaget's Developmental Psychology, Routledge and Kegan Paul.

BENNETS, T. (1981) Progression in the Geography Curriculum, in WALFORD, R. (ed) Signposts for Geography Teaching, Longman.

BLAUT, J.M. and STEA, D. (1971) Studies in Geographic Learning, Annals of the Association of American Geographers, vol.61, Reprinted in BALE, J., GRAVES, N. and WALFORD, R. (eds) Perspectives in Geographical Education, Oliver and Boyd.

BOARDMAN, D. (1974) Objectives and Constraints in Geographical Fieldwork, Journal of Curriculum Studies, vol.6, no.2.

BIBLIOGRAPHY

BOARDMAN, D. (1976a) Graphicacy in the Curriculum, Educational Review, vol.28, no.2.

BOARDMAN, D. (1976b) Developing a Curriculum Unit, Teaching Geography, vol.2, no.1.

BOARDMAN, D. (1977) Evaluating Computer Assisted Learning, The Times Educational Supplement, 11 November.

BOARDMAN, D. (1978) Implications of a Modular Curriculum, Teaching Geography, vol.3, no.4.

BOARDMAN, D. (1979) Improving Simulation through Fieldwork, Teaching Geography, vol.4. no.4.

BOARDMAN, D. and ROBINSON, R. (1979) How Data can help in the Sixth Form, Teaching Geography, vol.4, no.3.

BOARDMAN, D. and TOWNER, E. (1979) Reading Ordnance Survey Maps: Some Problems of Graphicacy, Teaching Research Unit, University of Birmingham.

BOARDMAN, D. (1980) Dissemination Strategies in Four Geography Curriculum Projects, Journal of Curriculum Studies, vol.12, no.2.

BOARDMAN, D. and TOWNER, E. (1980) Problems of Correlating Air Photographs with Ordnance Survey Maps, Teaching Geography, vol.6, no.2.

BOARDMAN, D. (1981a) Progression in Geography Teaching, The Times Educational Supplement, 10 April.

BOARDMAN, D. (1981b) How Computers can aid Learning, Teaching Geography, vol.6, no.4.

BOARDMAN, D. (1981c) Geography in the 5-13 Curriculum, Teaching Geography, vol.7, no.2.

BOARDMAN, D. (ed) (1981d) GYSL with the Disadvantaged, The Geographical Association.

BOARDMAN, D. (1982a) Graphicacy through Landscape Models, Studies in Design Education Craft and Technology, vol.14, no.2.

BOARDMAN, D. (ed) (1982b) Geography with Slow Learners, The Geographical Association.

BREARLEY, M. and HITCHFIELD, E. (1966) A Teacher's Guide to Reading Piaget, Routledge and Kegan Paul.

BIBLIOGRAPHY

CATLING, S.J. (1978a) The Child's Spatial Conception and
     Geographic Education, Journal of Geography, vol.77, no.1.

CATLING, S.J. (1978b) Cognitive Mapping Exercises as a Primary
     Geographical Experience, Teaching Geography, vol.3, no.3.

CATLING, S.J. (1979) Maps and Cognitive Maps: the Young Child's
     Perception, Geography, vol.64, pt.4.

CATLING, S.J. (1980) Map Use and Objectives for Map Learning,
     Teaching Geography, vol.6, no.1.

CHARLTON, K.E. (1975) A Study of Pupil Understanding of Map
     Symbolism, Scale, Direction and Location in the Age Range
     8-13 Years, unpublished M.Phil. thesis, University of
     Leeds.

COLEMAN, A. (ed) (1982) Patterns on the Map, The Geographical
     Association.

DALE, P.F. (1971) Children's Reactions to Maps and Aerial
     Photographs, Area, vol.3, no.3.

DESIGN COUNCIL (1980) Design Education at Secondary Level,
     Design Council.

DONALDSON, M. (1978) Children's Minds, Fontana/Collins.

EGGLESTON, J. (1976) Developments in Design Education, Open
     Books.

FIELDEN, J. and PEARSON, P.K. (1978) The Cost of Learning with
     Computers, Council for Educational Technology.

FOX, P. (1981) Murderer at Large!, in WALFORD, R. (ed) Sign-
     posts for Geography Teaching, Longman.

FURTH, H.G. (1970) Piaget for Teachers, Prentice-Hall.

GEOGRAPHICAL ASSOCIATION (1981) Geography in the School
     Curriculum 5-16.

GERBER, R. and WILSON, P.S. (1979) Spatial Reference Systems
     and Mapping with Eleven-Year-Old Pupils, Geographical
     Education, vol.3,no.3.

GERBER, R. (1981a) Young Children's Understanding of the
     Elements of Maps, Teaching Geography, vol.6, no.2.

BIBLIOGRAPHY

GERBER, R. (1981b) Factors Affecting the Competence and
    Performance in Map Language of Children at the Concrete
    Level of Map Reasoning, Geographical Education, vol.4, no.1.

GRAVES, N.J. (1975) Geography in Education, Heinemann.

GRAVES, N.J. (1979) Curriculum Planning in Geography, Heinemann.

GRAVES, N.J. (1980) Geographical Education in Secondary Schools,
    The Geographical Association.

HEAMON, A.J. (1973) The Maturation of Spatial Ability in
    Geography, Educational Research, vol.16, no.1.

HOOPER, R. (1977) The National Development Programme in
    Computer Assisted Learning: Final Report of the Director,
    Council for Educational Technology.

HUTCHINGS, G.E. (1960) Landscape Drawing, Methuen.

INNER LONDON EDUCATION AUTHORITY (1981) The Study of Places in
    the Primary School.

MACDONALD, B. and WALKER, R. (1976) Changing the Curriculum,
    Open Books.

MACDONALD, B., ATKIN, R., JENKINS, D. and KEMMIS, S. (1977)
    Computer Assisted Learning: its Educational Potential,
    in HOOPER, R. The National Development Programme in
    Computer Assisted Learning: Final Report of the Director,
    Council for Educational Technology.

MACFARLANE-SMITH, I. (1964) Spatial Ability: Its Educational
    and Social Significance, University of London Press.

MCNALLY, D.W. (1973) Piaget, Education and Teaching, The
    Harvester Press.

MILLS, D. (ed) (1981) Geographical Work in Primary and Middle
    Schools, The Geographical Association.

MORPURGO, M. (1979) All Around the Year, John Murray.

NOYES, L. (1979) Are Some Maps better than Others?, Geography,
    vol.64, pt.4.

PALMER, J.A. (1981) The Contribution of an Integrated
    Environmental Studies Curriculum to the Development of
    Creativity in Primary School Children, unpublished M.Ed.
    dissertation, University of Birmingham.

BIBLIOGRAPHY

PALMER, J.A. and WISE, M.J. (1982) The Good, the Bad and the Ugly, The Geographical Association.

PEEL, E.A. (1971) The Nature of Adolescent Judgment, Staples Press.

PIAGET, J. and INHELDER, B. (1956) The Child's Conception of Space, Routledge and Kegan Paul.

PIAGET, J., INHELDER, B. and SZEMINSKA (1960) The Child's Conception of Geometry, Routledge and Kegan Paul.

PIAGET, J. (1971) Science of Education and the Psychology of the Child, Longman.

RAWLING, E. (1981a) Local Issues and Enquiry-Based Learning, Schools Council Geography 16-19 Project.

RAWLING, E. (1981b) More Shops for Abingdon!, in WALFORD, R. (ed) Signposts for Geography Teaching, Longman.

RICHMOND, P.G. (1970) An Introduction to Piaget, Routledge and Kegan Paul.

ROBINSON, A.H. and PETCHENIK, B.B. (1976) The Nature of Maps, University of Chicago Press.

ROBINSON, R., BOARDMAN, D., FENNER, J. and BLACKBURN, J.D. (1978, 1979) Data in Geography: Cities; Drainage Basins; Rural Landscapes; People and Work, Longman Resources Unit.

ROBINSON, R. (1981) Quantification and School Geography: a Clarification, in WALFORD, R. (ed) Signposts for Geography Teaching, Longman.

SALT, C.D. (1971) An Investigation into the Ability of 11-12 Year-Old Pupils to read and understand Maps, unpublished M.A. thesis, University of Sheffield.

SANDFORD, H.A. (1967) An Experimental Investigation into Children's Perception of a School Atlas Map, unpublished M.Phil. thesis, University of London.

SANDFORD, H.A. (1970) A study of the Concepts involved in the Reading and Interpretation of Atlases by Secondary School Children, unpublished Ph.D. thesis, University of London.

SANDFORD, H.A. (1972) Perceptual Problems, in GRAVES, N. (ed) New Movements in the Study and Teaching of Geography, Temple Smith.

BIBLIOGRAPHY

SANDFORD, H.A. (1978) Taking a Fresh Look at Atlases,
    Teaching Geography, vol.4, no.2.

SANDFORD, H.A. (1979) Things Maps don't tell us, Geography,
    vol.64, pt.4.

SATTERLY, D.J. (1964) Skills and Concepts involved in Map
    Drawing and Interpretation, New Era, no.45. Reprinted in
    BALE, J., GRAVES, N. and WALFORD, R. (eds) (1973)
    Perspectives in Geographical Education, Oliver and Boyd.

SCHOOLS COUNCIL (1974, 1975) Geography for the Young School
    Leaver: Man, Land, and Leisure; Cities and People; People,
    Place and Work, Nelson.

SCHOOLS COUNCIL (1978, 1980) Geography 14-18: Urban Geography;
    Industry; Population; Transport Networks; Water and Rivers,
    Macmillan Education.

SCHOOLS COUNCIL (1979) Computers in the Curriculum: Geography,
    Longman Resources Unit.

SHEPHERD, I.D.H. (1976) Hunt the Hurkle, Computers in Geography
    Study Group, Middlesex Polytechnic.

SHEPHERD, I.D.H., COOPER, Z.A. and WALKER, D.R.F. (1980)
    Computer Assisted Learning in Geography: Current Trends
    and Future Prospects, Council for Educational Technology
    with the Geographical Association.

SIMMONS, R.L. and MEARS, J.K. (1977) Landscape Drawing: A
    Neglected Aspect of Graphicacy, Teaching Geography
    Occasional Paper No.29, The Geographical Association.

TAYLOR, J.L. and WALFORD, R. (1972) Simulation in the Classroom,
    Penguin.

TIDSWELL, V. (1972) The Herefordshire Farm Game, in TAYLOR, J.L.
    and WALFORD, R. Simulation in the Classroom, Penguin.

TIDSWELL, V. (1981) The Overlap between School and University
    Geography, in WALFORD, R. (ed) Signposts for Geography
    Teaching, Longman.

TOLLEY, H. and REYNOLDS, J.B. (1977) Geography 14-18: A Hand-
    book for School-Based Curriculum Development, Macmillan
    Education.

WALFORD, R. (ed) (1981) Signposts for Geography Teaching,
    Longman.

Index

INDEX

INDEX

INDEX

66805

DATE DUE

GAYLORD